# Conglomerate Mergers

# Conglomerate Mergers

## Causes, Consequences, and Remedies

### George J. Benston

American Enterprise Institute for Public Policy Research
Washington, D.C.

George J. Benston is a professor of accounting, economics, and finance at the Graduate School of Management, The University of Rochester. Dr. Benston is a member of the editorial boards of several academic journals. He is the author of over fifty scholarly articles and monographs in his fields. His books include *Corporate Financial Disclosure in the UK and the USA* (1976) and *Contemporary Cost Accounting and Control* (1970 and 1977).

Library of Congress Cataloging in Publication Data

Benston, George J
  Conglomerate mergers.

  (AEI studies ; 270)
  Bibliography: p.
  1. Consolidation and merger of corporations—
United States.   2. Conglomerate corporations—United
States.   I. Title.   II. Series: American Enterprise
Institute for Public Policy Research.   AEI studies ;
270.
HD2741.B39        338.8'3'0973        80-12017
ISBN 0-8447-3373-3

AEI Studies 270

*Printed in the United States of America*

# CONTENTS

# ACKNOWLEDGMENTS

I received valuable suggestions and editorial help from, particularly, Yale Brozen, Julian Franks, Salem Katsh, and Jeffrey Kessler, and also from Betty Bock, Michael Bradley, and Alfred Rappaport. An earlier version of this study was prepared for and presented to the Subcommittee on Antitrust and Monopoly of the Senate Judiciary Committee on May 17, 1979, as testimony on pending legislation that would restrict merger activity. This earlier version was sponsored by the Business Roundtable, whose financial support is gratefully acknowledged. The Roundtable did not direct or control in any way the contents of this testimony or of the present study, and it does not necessarily concur with the conclusions or any other part of the paper. In addition, those mentioned above, who kindly provided me with their suggestions, should not be considered responsible for or necessarily in agreement with this study.

G.J.B.

# SUMMARY AND OVERVIEW

Mergers provide an important part of the market for corporate assets and contribute to making capital markets efficient. They are a means by which (1) entrepreneurs are rewarded for their success and diversify their portfolios; (2) economic organizations are restructured into more efficient combinations; (3) investment capital flows into areas of the economy where it is needed; (4) corporate assets are purchased and sold; (5) risks in supplying capital to small and medium-sized businesses are reduced and capital formation thereby encouraged; and (6) poor managers of publicly owned corporations are displaced. Mergers are also a means of corporate growth, a fact of concern to those who oppose large firm size generally. But largeness reduces the cost of raising capital, produces lower-risk outlets for the placement of capital desired by savers and investors, and makes it possible to extend the use of capital-intensive technologies. Since section 7 of the Clayton Act as amended by the 1950 Celler-Kefauver Act blocks most horizontal and large vertical mergers (combinations of similar businesses or of companies that are major traders with each other), the conglomerate merger (a combination of businesses that are not clearly related) is one of the few avenues to the creation of large firms by means more rapid than internal growth.

The benefits and costs of mergers are the principal subjects of this study. The reasons for the current merger "wave" are discussed in chapter 1. Among the various explanations that have been put forth, two appear to be most important. One is the fact that mergers are desirable for many companies because of advances in technology and changes in demand for products. As a consequence of these changes, the assets of some companies are worth more when managed by an

1

acquiring company than they are under the managers of the acquired company.

The second explanation for the current merger "wave" is that tax and regulatory policies have made corporate purchases of companies a preferable means of investment. Inflation-induced increases in the personal income tax have made dividends less valuable for stockholders and have encouraged the retention of earnings. And corporate income taxes, combined with inflation and the implicit taxes imposed by government regulation, have decreased the market value of the shares of many corporations to less than the replacement value of their assets, so that whole firms are often a bargain in the marketplace under their current management. Thus, as analysis below shows, in today's economic environment shareholders of both acquiring and acquired companies frequently benefit from a merger.

The motivations for and consequences of mergers are analyzed in chapter 2. These include the benefits to entrepreneurs and small business persons, who look to mergers as a possible reward for their enterprise. Thus, mergers encourage the founding of new businesses. The data presented show that mergers have not adversely affected small businesses; on the contrary, if mergers are impeded legislatively, small business and the benefits to the economy from entrepreneurship will be diminished.

Next in chapter 2 the consequences of mergers are analyzed generally from the standpoint of shareholders. I find that monopoly profits are of no importance as a motivation for conglomerate mergers; neither do such profits occur as a result of conglomerate mergers. But I show that the achievement of production, marketing, financing, and other economies, the purchase and sale of managerial and other talents and resources made available by mergers, and the preferability of mergers as investments for corporations with strong cash flows, are important considerations. In addition, the displacement of poor managers is an important private inducement for and socially useful consequence of some mergers. The available empirical studies that measure the benefits and costs of mergers to shareholders support the conclusion that mergers lead to efficient resource allocation; they show that shareholders of acquired companies receive a considerable increase in the market price of their shares, while shareholders of acquiring companies receive either normal or higher-than-normal returns.

The motivations of managers toward mergers also are considered in chapter 2. Critics have claimed that managers of large conglomerates have emphasized growth at the expense of their shareholders' interests. Neither reasoning nor data, however, support this assertion. The analy-

2

sis shows that the motivations for and consequences of mergers are beneficial on the average; these conclusions are supported by the available empirical research.

In chapter 3 the consequences of mergers to society are considered. Mergers tend to benefit consumers since they often enhance efficiency. There also is reason to believe that workers and communities benefit from mergers. Unfortunately, there is little significant research on the social and political impact of large firms generally (and conglomerate mergers in particular). This type of research should be encouraged, and should be concluded before legislation predicated on noneconomic considerations is proposed and enacted.

Critics nevertheless have pointed to the aggregate concentration ratio (ACR) as evidence that mergers enhance centralized business power to the possible detriment of our democracy or the pluralism of our society. However, on examination, I find that these statistics are numerically and conceptually invalid. Moreover, the ACR does not show increasing levels of aggregate concentration. A closer and more direct analysis of business power shows that few corporations have unwarranted discretionary power. If "power" is a meaningful concern, its full dimensions should be examined, including the "power" of government, of small business, of labor, and of the consumer, in addition to that of big business.

Finally, the available and proposed remedies for undesirable mergers are analyzed in chapter 4. The costs of administering any governmental ban on large mergers are likely to be substantial. The apparently strict *per se* rules that are proposed actually would be subject to varied interpretations and to avoidance, a process that could impose material costs on society. The most important costs, however, would be the denial of the beneficial aspects of mergers.

The study concludes with a review of the arguments put forth by the U.S. Department of Justice in support of legislation that would severely restrict conglomerate mergers. I find that these arguments are without foundation in fact or logic. Therefore, I conclude that new antimerger legislation is ill-advised. It would bar rational merger activity which provides substantial benefits. In addition, it would impose significant new costs on society without producing new, compensating benefits.

# 1
## The Reasons for the Current Merger "Wave"

### Merger Volume since 1895

Legislative and public concern about mergers appears to be a function of the volume of mergers. This volume has varied considerably over the period 1895–1977, as shown in figure 1.[1] Several merger "waves" are commonly identified: the 1899 and 1901 peaks are associated with horizontal mergers that gave birth to the great trusts, many of which were short-lived.[2] The late 1920s wave is rarely mentioned. But, according to F. M. Scherer, who compiled and plotted the data in figure 1, the late 1940s boomlet prompted Congress to pass the Celler-Kefauver Act.[3] The late 1960s wave, which reached a peak in 1968, was characterized by conglomerate mergers, combinations of diverse enterprises that were not considered horizontal (similar businesses) or vertical (links in the chain from raw material to manufacture to final sale) mergers. These, in turn, gave rise to another wave of publications and demands for legislation to control or prevent such mergers. The latest so-called merger wave has spawned legislative proposals such as S. 600 (The Small and Independent Business Protection Act of 1979) that would severely restrict combinations of large corporations.

Although it may be the best historical series available, figure 1 nevertheless presents a somewhat misleading picture of merger activity

[1] F. M. Scherer, "Prepared Statement," in U.S. Congress, Senate, Subcommittee on Antitrust, Monopoly, and Business Rights, *Mergers and Economic Concentration: Hearings on S. 600*, 96th Congress, 1st session, May 17, 1979, pp. 135–142.

[2] However, see Carl Eis, "The 1919–1930 Merger Movement in American Industry," *Journal of Law and Economics* 12 (October 1969): 267–296.

[3] Scherer states that the figure "is the first historically consistent series on the volume of U.S. merger activity back to the late 19th century" (Senate, Subcommittee on Antitrust, Monopoly, and Business Rights, *Mergers*, p. 134).

# FIGURE 1

## Volume of Manufacturing and Mining Firm Acquisitions, 1895–1977

Value of Acquired Firms

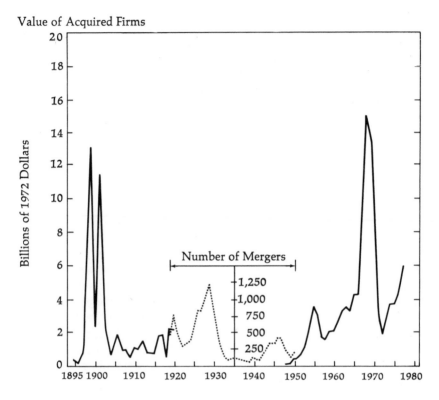

SOURCE: Scherer, "Prepared Statement," in Senate, Subcommittee on Antitrust, Monopoly, and Business Rights, *Mergers and Economic Concentration: Hearings on S. 600*, Figure 1, p. 135. Scherer states that "the sources of the table were as follows: For 1895-1920, Ralph L. Nelson, 'Merger Movements in American Industry, 1895-1956' (Princeton University Press: 1959), p. 37; for 1919-39, Willard L. Thorp, 'The Merger Movement,' in Temporary National Economic Committee Monograph No. 27, 'The Structure of Industry' (Washington: 1941), p. 233; for 1940-50, U.S. House of Representatives, Select Committee on Small Business, Staff Report, 'Mergers and Superconcentration' (Washington: 1962); and for 1948-77, Federal Trade Commission, 'Statistical Report on Mergers and Acquisitions' (Washington: November 1977), p. 100. The Nelson and FTC series [solid lines] are in terms of the dollar value of assets acquired or merged; the Thorp and Small Business Committee series [dotted lines] are (undoubtedly incomplete) counts of the numbers of mergers. The dollar series have been converted to constant 1972 dollar values using a composite price deflator or (earlier) the all-commodity Wholesale Price Index, 20 percent to nonresidential construction or (earlier) construction materials, and 27 percent to producers' durable equipment or (earlier) industrial machinery" (p. 134).

in the United States. Two good features should be mentioned initially. Scherer's use of constant dollars avoids the error found in many such charts in which the rise in dollar volume of mergers appears greater than it is because of the spectacular increase in inflation during the last two decades. His use of dollar volumes also avoids the error of charts that give mergers in terms of the number over $10 million. In these, the number of mergers increases solely because the cutoff line is lowered as inflation makes $10 million less in real terms. But the data presented in figure 1 do not account for the growth of the economy. Although the constant dollar volume of mergers was greater in 1968 than in 1898 and 1901, so was the asset size of the mining and manufacturing sector and of the economy. Indeed, when we consider that the economy was over thirteen times larger (in constant dollars) in 1968 than in 1898, the contemporary merger waves are of considerably smaller relative magnitudes. In addition, the size of the mining and manufacturing sector in relation to the economy has been shrinking. Therefore, even figures as carefully constructed as figure 1 tend to overstate considerably the magnitude of contemporary merger activity. Indeed, if the data were scaled appropriately, what appears as a wave would be seen as a mere ripple.

Since the current merger activity has been characterized graphically as a wave about which the public should be concerned, it is desirable to consider why a wave, real or apparent, should be occurring. This is the task of the present chapter; the next chapter considers the reasons for mergers generally.

Several explanations for the current merger wave are possible. These include the following suggestions: (1) accounting procedures are used that mislead investors, thereby motivating promoters and managers to bring about mergers; (2) conglomerate mergers in particular are motivated by legislation prohibiting other types of mergers (and mergers in general) by the threat of additional antimerger legislation; (3) growth and changes in enterprises bring these enterprises to a stage in their development at which mergers are rational; (4) economic disturbances change relative perceptions about the value of companies, which leads to an increase in trading; and (5) mergers are attractive investments for acquiring companies, owing to the present economic and tax climate.

## Misleading Accounting Procedures

Some writers claim that accounting procedures which misled the public were a causal factor in many conglomerate mergers of the 1960s.

7

Abraham J. Briloff,[4] among others,[5] is a principal proponent of this theory. In a number of articles that appeared in scholarly journals and in *Barron's*, he (and others) claimed that conglomerates were misleading the public with accounting procedures that made their earnings appear to increase. One procedure cited was that of adding the earnings of an acquired company to the earnings of the acquiring company, which increased the conglomerate's reported annual earnings even when the acquisition was consummated toward the end of the year. These writers claimed that the unwary might believe that the higher earnings were due to the improved operations of the acquirer.

A second method noted was that of acquiring a company with a lower ratio of share prices per dollar of earnings. The earnings of the acquired company were added to the acquiring company's earnings, which, allegedly, unsuspecting investors multiplied by the acquiring company's higher price/earnings ratio to determine a price for the merged company's shares. A third accounting "device" criticized was that of using the pooling-of-interests method instead of the purchase method of accounting for an acquisition. Under the pooling-of-interests method the acquiring company simply adds the book values of the acquired company to its own book values. Any difference between the market value of the acquiring company's shares and the book value of the acquired company for which they were exchanged is not recorded. Under the purchase method the difference is recorded as goodwill and it is amortized against earnings over time (usually forty years). Thus, annual reported earnings will be biased upward where the pooling-of-interests method is used. Briloff (and others) have asserted that these accounting procedures encouraged mergers (particularly by conglomerates), to the detriment of investors.

The validity of this claim obviously rests on the assumption that investors were, in fact, misled. A number of empirical studies have been conducted which find that voluntarily chosen accounting alternatives do not affect share prices; the stock market is not that easily fooled.[6] In particular, a study by Hai Hong, Robert S. Kaplan, and

---

[4] Abraham J. Briloff, "Accounting Practices and the Merger Movement," *Notre Dame Lawyer* 45 (Summer 1970): 604–628.

[5] Many articles have been published on methods of accounting for mergers and their role as motivating factors. See, for example, articles in *St. John's Law Review* 44 (Spring 1970, Special Edition), and Peter O. Steiner, *Mergers: Motives, Effects, Policies* (Ann Arbor: University of Michigan Press, 1975), Chapter 5.

[6] Many of these studies are reviewed in George J. Benston, *Corporate Financial Disclosure in the UK and the USA* (Lexington, Mass.: Lexington Books, D. C. Heath & Company, 1976), Chapter 4.

Gershon Mandelker[7] examined one aspect of the relationship between accounting practices and mergers—the assertion that pooling-of-interests accounting misled investors. They compared the behavior of the share prices of companies that used this method of accounting for mergers with that of the share prices of companies that used the purchase method. (Other changes attributable to general stock market conditions were adjusted for statistically.) They found no significant difference between the groups, which is inconsistent with the hypothesis that investors were misled.

In any event, the accounting rules were tightened substantially by the American Institute of Certified Public Accountants, the Financial Accounting Standards Board, and the Securities Exchange Commission. The new disclosure and documentation requirements have eliminated any reason to believe that investors have been misled in recent years or are being misled now. Therefore, I reject this theory as an explanation of the current merger wave.

## Enacted and Proposed Antimerger Legislation

The 1950 amendment to the Clayton Act (the Celler-Kefauver Act) has barred many horizontal and vertical mergers that would otherwise have occurred. Peter O. Steiner did a careful analysis of the Federal Trade Commission (FTC) merger reports from 1948 through 1972. He distinguishes product extension from pure conglomerate mergers and concludes that "the importance of conglomerate mergers has increased since 1950, a date whose significance lies in the passage of the Celler-Kefauver Amendments to the Clayton Act, which put real teeth into the antimerger provisions of Section 7 of that Act."[8] He explains further:

> The differences in *level* [of the number of conglomerate mergers] seem to me almost wholly explained by the antitrust climate. Large vertical mergers had become vulnerable by the late sixties. The same was true for horizontal and market extension mergers in general, but the willingness of the Justice Department to permit major mergers among leading oil companies was an important exception. Thus the only large mergers that were not relatively sure to invite

[7] Hai Hong, Robert S. Kaplan, and Gershon Mandelker, "Pooling vs. Purchase: The Effect of Accounting for Mergers on Stock Prices," *Accounting Review* 53 (January 1978): 31–47.

[8] Steiner, *Mergers*, pp. 22–23.

Justice Department response were in the conglomerate categories—and the purer the better.[9]

As is shown further below, the benefits from mergers in general are such that, if some types of mergers are blocked, others (such as the pure conglomerate merger) will arise.

Proposed new antimerger acts may themselves be partly responsible for the magnitude of the current merger wave. Some companies that were merely contemplating mergers are said to have undertaken them more quickly because of the possibility that additional antimerger legislation would be passed.[10] As a consequence, the yearly number of mergers effected is enhanced. Therefore, from data showing increased merger activity during late 1978 or 1979 one should not draw the inference that such an increase necessarily would continue in the absence of threatened legislation.

## Growth of and Changes in Enterprises

A substantial part of what appear to be cycles or waves of mergers may simply be the natural outcome of changes over time in technology, demand, or other economic factors. These apparent cycles or waves could also be a manifestation of an essentially random process.

As I discuss in detail in chapter 2, mergers are frequently the outcome of the normal growth of many enterprises. That is, in the life cycle of an enterprise, after its beginning as a successful, entrepreneurial venture, the best possible further development may take the form of a merger with another enterprise. Companies may seek mergers because they have reached the point at which technological, distributional, financing, or managerial developments make a combination with another, usually larger, company economically desirable. Larger companies may want to acquire or otherwise combine with other firms because their own internal expansion has become impossible or less profitable than acquisitions, or because they seek a larger vehicle for their managerial or technical talents or a larger market for their products.

Many of the factors that motivate the establishment, development, and combination of enterprises are likely to be exogenous forces that affect whole segments of the economy at about the same time and that manifest themselves—among other ways—in the form of periodic episodes of heightened merger activity. To be sure, at this time we

---

[9] Ibid., pp. 23–26 (footnote omitted, emphasis in original).

[10] From conversations with investment bankers and consultants.

understand little of this process from an empirical standpoint. But it does seem appropriate to conclude that, although mergers may occur in waves, the grouping is not necessarily a consequence of a lemming-like "urge to merge" among companies generally.

The wavelike appearance of the statistics also could be due, in part at least, to changes in the simple outcome of a random series of merger activities over time. As statisticians know, even though a series of changes is generated by a random process, the levels (sums) of such a series, when graphed, will give the appearance of waves. For example, the changes in the levels of stock market prices over time have been shown to be randomly distributed; when these random changes are summed to produce levels, and graphed, they appear as waves, perhaps suggesting systematic influences where none exist. This may also be the case for a portion of the merger series.

### Economic Disturbances

One company is purchased by another or shares of companies are exchanged because people place different values on assets. In the case of any asset that is used for production, a trade occurs because of differently perceived values. Each party considers itself to be better off despite the transactions costs that each must incur.

Michael Gort[11] proposed the theory that economic disturbances, such as a technological change or a rapid rate of increase in business opportunities and stock prices, cause the managers of some firms to believe that buying other firms offers a higher rate of return than further direct investment in their own firms, perhaps because the other firms are in industries that have better profit and growth prospects. The owners of the other firms, however, do not value these possibilities as highly. Therefore, mergers and purchases of companies occur. In a test of his theory with data from the years 1951 through 1959, Gort dismissed as explanatory factors attempts to monopolize or (in large measure) to achieve economies of scale.[12] Heterogeneous expectations or beliefs, however, did appear to be important.

---

[11] Michael Gort, "An Economic Disturbance Theory of Mergers," *Quarterly Journal of Economics* 83 (November 1969): 624–642.

[12] However, Steiner (*Mergers*, p. 199) argues that Gort's data can be read to indicate that achievement of economies of scale is an important factor. Also, a study by Weiss concludes that, on the average, 83 to 91 percent of the assets acquired in six industries between 1929 and 1958 were of suboptimal scale. In the 1948–1958 period, 100 percent of the capacity acquired by the four major companies in five industries and 62 percent in the sixth were of suboptimal scale. (Leonard W. Weiss, "An Evaluation of Mergers in Six Industries," *Review of Economics and Statistics* 47 (May 1965): 177.

Although the present period is not characterized by a rising stock market or by dramatic technological changes, the "disturbance" theory may provide an explanation for some recent mergers. A sudden increase in government regulation and other disturbing economic factors (such as rising competition from foreign sources and decreasing tariffs) might be considered negative technological changes that give rise to decreased share prices as a consequence of pessimism among many investors about prospects for future cash flows. Corporate officers may not share this opinion and they may, therefore, consider shares to be undervalued. Hence, they conclude that an acquisition, even at a premium over current share prices, is a good investment of their shareholders' resources.[13] This version of the disturbance theory is considered further in the next section.

### Mergers as Preferable Investments for Acquiring Companies

By far the most important single factor accounting for the current so-called merger wave is the clear preference of some companies in today's economic climate for mergers over other forms of investment. A feature of current merger activity is the acquisition of companies by the purchase of their owners' shares for cash as compared with the exchanges of stock common in the 1960s. A major part of this phenomenon may be explained in terms of governmental actions (including taxation) affecting the returns to investments made by corporations for their shareholders. In essence, the higher cost caused by increased governmental regulation in the 1970s, together with the increase in corporate and personal taxes brought about by inflation, has in many cases made the acquisition of a company for cash the most easily justifiable investment—and perhaps the only justifiable one.

It should be remembered that the acquisition of a corporation by a tender offer or other purchase of shares for cash is simply an investment. As is the case with any other investment, the acquiring corporation's management calculates the investment's present value by estimating the net cash flows that are expected to be derived from it (including the savings that will be made by combining operations, distribution, managements, etc.), and discounting the flows by an appropriate interest rate. This investment is then compared with alternatives.[14]

---

[13] This insight is due to Alfred Rappaport (in conversation).

[14] See Alfred Rappaport, "Strategic Analysis for More Profitable Acquisitions," *Harvard Business Review* 57 (July–August 1979): 99–110, for a description of the relevant variables and methodology.

In particular, let us consider the situation that arises when a corporation must decide how to invest a relatively large cash amount that it has acquired as a consequence of shifts in the economic demand for its products. One alternative is to distribute cash dividends to the shareholders. However, if dividends are increased shareholders will be faced with paying personal tax on the amounts received; this tax, of course, is *in addition* to the corporate income taxes which will already have been paid. As inflation has increased nominal incomes, shareholders (and others) have been pushed into higher marginal tax brackets. For example, the average shareholder who had a gross income of $11,000 in 1966, and a taxable net income of $7,500 (after the 10 percent standard deduction and $2,400 for four exemptions), was in the 19 percent marginal tax bracket (that is, additional dividend income would be taxed at 19 percent). By 1975, inflation had pushed that same taxpayer's gross income to $18,215—if we assume unchanged real income—and taxable net income to $12,301 (after the 16 percent standard deduction and $3,000 for four exemptions). The marginal tax rate for additional dividend income for this taxpayer is now 25 percent. Even if this shareholder could invest the cash received as dividends to yield a 10 percent return, the shareholder would be better off if the corporation kept the funds and invested them at any rate after corporate income tax exceeding 7.5 percent. Thus, distributing additional dividends is very often less advantageous for shareholders than putting those funds into corporate investment opportunities.

Another alternative for the corporation is to return funds to the shareholders by buying back shares in the market. But again, the shareholders' personal income taxes will reduce the benefit of this "investment." Moreover, even if a capital gains treatment is accepted by the Internal Revenue Service,[15] since inflation has increased the nominal values of many shares in relation to their original purchase price, the nominal gain is still likely to be considerable. This makes its realization undesirable for many shareholders. The "gain" to many shareholders, on which they have been taxed, has actually turned out to be fictitious.[16] In addition, when payouts of cash would decrease the size of the company significantly, the distribution is likely to injure

---

[15] While gains from a sale of stock are ordinarily afforded capital gains treatment, the Internal Revenue Code treats certain redemptions as dividends, subject to tax as ordinary income. See Internal Revenue Code § 302(d).

[16] For a full discussion and analysis, see Martin Feldstein and Lawrence Summers, *Inflation and Taxation of Capital Income in the Corporate Sector*, Working Paper No. 312, National Bureau of Economic Research, January 1979.

shareholders. A shrinking enterprise offers constrained opportunities for employees and for adjustment of operations to meet economic changes. As a consequence, a corporation that reduces its size is likely to face higher wage and capital costs and to lose its more dynamic and enterprising managers who see little future in working for such a business. Therefore, retentions by the corporation generally offer better returns to shareholders than do payouts.

Funds may be invested within the corporation's industry, but this type of investment may not be economically justifiable for a number of reasons. The industry may have underutilized capacity or be at a mature stage where substantial new investment or additional capacity is not warranted. It may be a cyclical industry from which diversification is desirable, as discussed below. An example is provided by the following description of the merger activities of Hershey Foods:

> With the heightened competition in the chocolate candy market and with cocoa bean prices at sky-high levels, Hershey Foods has been unable to show any earnings improvement in recent years. Its management countered with a diversification program. Two acquisitions were completed in the first quarter [1979]. It acquired Friendly Ice Cream, a large well established restaurant chain for $158 million, and then acquired Skinner Macaroni. Following the two acquisitions, Hershey's non-candy sales account for 36 percent of total revenues.[17]

A dominant company, moreover, may fear that antitrust attacks will follow from new investments tending to maintain or increase its market share. For example, the Federal Trade Commission has brought a complaint against DuPont to prevent it from keeping a plant it is building to produce additional titanium dioxide on the ground that it is a dominant firm in the titanium dioxide industry with 40 percent of the domestic market.[18]

In some cases a corporation may expect a negative present value on investments in its industry because the government has placed a special tax or regulatory burden on that industry.[19] In June 1978, for ex-

---

[17] "Mergers on Parade," *Mergers and Acquisitions* 14 (Spring 1979): 50. Similar descriptions can be found in this and almost every other issue of this publication.

[18] "In the Matter of E. I. DuPont de Nemours and Co., a Corporation, Docket No. 9108," *CCH Trade Regulation Reporter, 1976–1979 FTC Complaints and Orders*, September 4, 1979, Paragraph 21,613.

[19] The Department of Energy, for example, does not permit oil companies to earn a return on their investment in refineries if it serves primarily to upgrade such products as heavy oils into gasoline.

ample, the Alaska legislature passed its thirteenth tax increase on oil companies in ten years. The result has been a decrease in the return on investment in expanding oil production to less than 9 percent—less than can be earned on government bonds; this has caused twenty-one oil companies to disband their exploration teams.[20]

Arthur Andersen & Co. has measured the costs of some of the principal government regulations imposed primarily in the 1970s.[21] This study assessed the incremental costs to forty-eight companies of complying with the regulatory requirements of six federal government agencies and programs: the Environmental Protection Agency (EPA), the Equal Employment Opportunity Commission (EEOC), the Occupational Safety and Health Administration (OSHA), the Department of Energy (DOE), the Employee Retirement Income Security Act (ERISA), and the Federal Trade Commission (FTC). The incremental costs for 1977 (those the companies would not otherwise have incurred)[22] totaled $2.6 billion for the forty-eight companies studied. These costs amounted to 17 percent of total capital expenditures, 43 percent of research and development costs, and 23 percent of net income after taxes. The largest costs were imposed by EPA (77 percent of the total), followed by EEOC (8 percent), OSHA (7 percent), and DOE (4 percent). These regulatory costs are the equivalent of a tax on the net cash flows that are expected from the labor and materials expended for investments in facilities, a tax which makes these investments economically inferior to other uses of the labor and materials. Indeed, in many instances these investments have become net-loss projects. Thus, in those industries in which such regulatory costs are particularly high, a large new investment in expansion will often represent a misuse of shareholder resources.

Another possible alternative to merger is direct (de novo) investment in another, or in a related, industry. In addition to the regulatory costs discussed above, these investments are subject to other drawbacks. The principal one is that de novo projects are often best undertaken by independent entrepreneurs who are able and willing to invest the required effort and skills and to undertake the large risks involved because they expect to garner the rewards. Should a large corporation undertake such a risky venture it would face serious problems. If the

---

[20] "The Great Alaskan Oil Freeze," *Business Week*, February 26, 1979, pp. 74–88.

[21] Arthur Andersen & Co., *Cost of Government Regulation Study for the Business Roundtable* (Chicago, Ill.: March 1979).

[22] Opportunity costs, such as changes in productivity, and the costs of delays caused by regulation, are not included, nor are the social benefits (if any) from regulation deducted.

15

venture is unsuccessful the company must nevertheless pay the salaries and expenses of the employees and must account to its shareholders for undertaking such a risk. If the venture is successful the large company will face the possibility that the employees involved will leave to set up their own businesses or will be dissatisfied because they get only a small share of the profits that, in their view, are due to their efforts. Consequently, it is often preferable for larger corporations to purchase established entrepreneurial ventures. Furthermore (as is discussed in chapter 2), a buyout is often very much desired and expected by successful entrepreneurs; indeed, it constitutes an important incentive for undertaking the risks involved in the first place.

It is important to note as well that de novo investments by large corporations in unrelated industries are often unlikely to be profitable because few corporations have the requisite knowledge for such undertakings. Personnel with the needed skills must be trained; plants must be constructed, equipment purchased and installed, distribution networks developed, advertising designed, and customer relations established, for example. It is often preferable, therefore, to purchase an existing enterprise in the unrelated industry.

Perhaps the most important motivation for many recent mergers is the advantage to the acquiring corporation of purchasing a corporation's shares as a means of buying its assets at a lower cost than that of new construction. Book and replacement costs higher than market values per share have been characteristic of markets in the 1970s. Melvin Krasney has calculated the ratios of book to market values per share for all companies whose financial statements are listed on Standard and Poor's Annual Compustat and CRSP Monthly tapes (a subset of New York Stock Exchange listed companies). From 1963 (the first year with sufficient data—over 500 companies) through 1969 the mean ratios (and standard deviations, in parentheses) ranged from 0.53 (0.31) to 0.79 (0.69). In 1970, 1971, and 1972 the mean ratios (and standard deviations) were 0.88 (0.66), 0.80 (0.61), and 0.81 (0.61). From 1972 through 1977 they ranged from 1.12 (0.69) to 1.92 (1.58).[23]

Book values higher than market values are very unusual because the accounting process normally tends to understate the present value of assets and equity reported on a balance sheet. Accountants follow rules that lead to the immediate writing off (expensing) of expenditures on intangible assets, such as research and development, adver-

---

[23] Melvin Krasney, "Research in Progress," University of Rochester, Rochester, N.Y., 1979.

tising, employee training, and goodwill. In addition, accounting data are not adjusted for inflation, and therefore long-term fixed assets and inventories tend to be understated at current price levels and long-term liabilities tend to be overstated. Therefore, stock market values, which are not bound by accounting rules, should exceed book values. The fact that on the average they did not from 1972 through 1977 (as Krasney's data show) is indicative of the significant depressing effect which governmental policies (or certain other factors) have had on economic earnings and on stock market prices.

Depressed stock market prices are due in part to the effects of inflation on corporate income taxes. Since expenses that are a consequence of using up fixed assets (for example, depreciation) are not deductible at amounts that reflect current price levels but rather at the price level that prevailed when the assets were purchased, inflation increases the income taxes corporations must pay. According to Feldstein and Summers's calculations:

> The overall effect of inflation with existing tax laws was to raise the 1977 tax burden on corporate sector capital income by more than $32 billion. . . . The extra tax raised the total tax burdens on nonfinancial corporate capital income by more than one-half of its noninflation value, raising the total effective tax rate from 43 percent to 66 percent. The substantial increase in the effective tax rate on capital used in the nonfinancial corporate sector can influence the performance of the economy in a number of important ways. The most obvious of these is a reduction in the rate of capital formation in response to the reduction in the real after tax return.[24]

Another obvious consequence of the higher effective corporate tax rate is a reduction in the market values of corporate shares.

When stock market values are below book values, which are already understated (in relation to replacement cost), a corporation that wishes to make a large investment in today's economic climate can frequently acquire assets at substantially less than their replacement values by purchasing the shares of companies rather than by purchasing the assets directly. Such purchases also have the advantage over de novo investments of saving the cost of start-ups. And it would be foolish to create assets that would add less to the market value of the corporation than their cost; that would guarantee an immediate loss.

---

[24] Feldstein and Summers, *Inflation and Taxation of Capital Income*, p. 47.

## Conclusions

In sum, several factors explain the current so-called merger wave. Of the five factors considered here, misleading accounting practices clearly are not applicable to the present period, whether or not they were relevant at an earlier date. The Celler-Kefauver Act, which made all large mergers subject to challenge except those considered relatively pure conglomerate mergers, appears responsible, in part, for the earlier wave of conglomerate mergers. Proposed legislation that would severely curtail mergers by large companies may explain some of the current increase in merger activity; what appears to be an increase in rate may be only a timing phenomenon. Some of the current merger activity also may simply be the natural outcome of exogenous technological or demand changes; and some of the activity may simply be the natural clustering of random occurrences. Of overriding significance, I believe, is the current economic climate, including the effect of regulatory costs and taxes on the desirability of alternative investment choices by corporations that have cash to invest and that want to diversify. These companies frequently find that a merger is the most productive investment opportunity available, and that alternative investments would not be economically justifiable.

# 2

# Motivations for and Consequences of Merger Activity

In this chapter the motivations for and consequences of merger activity are discussed with respect to both the acquiring and the acquired businesses. The chapter focuses particularly on shareholders and managers and also considers the interests of other beneficiaries of merger activity as causal factors. In the first part of this chapter, however, I note several relevant supply and demand factors and then analyze merger activity from the standpoint of its importance to the small entrepreneur—why small businesses in particular would be adversely affected by a significant restraint on the market for companies.

## General Supply and Demand Factors

In essence, a merger represents a purchase and sale of a company. Like any other such transaction, it is governed by supply and demand, as constrained by laws and institutions and the associated costs they impose. Therefore, if we are to reach conclusions about the effects and usefulness of mergers, we should inquire first about the factors that cause mergers to occur—the motivations that underlie the supply of and demand for companies.

Mergers are voluntary transactions—shareholders vote or tender their shares. The motivations underlying mergers, therefore, are related to the net benefits that the respective parties expect to achieve.

## Smaller, Nonpublic Companies

Smaller, nonpublic companies are significantly and negatively affected by legislation that restricts mergers, even by legislation that appears to affect only larger companies. In the short run it might seem that limitations on the acquisition of large companies (such as those with over $350 million in sales or assets) would tend to increase the demand for the smaller companies which do not meet those criteria. If substantial classes of mergers are prohibited, however, the effect on smaller companies clearly will be negative over time. Smaller companies will be discouraged from growing, from being innovative, and from competing—in short, from essaying to become large companies. Their marketplace success, paradoxically, will mean financial loss— an inability to realize through sale the value of their enterprise. Moreover, those who do sell out or merge will receive less than they otherwise would, since the acquiring company's growth potential (or its sellout potential if it is smaller than some cutoff point) will be constrained with each acquisition it makes.

A restriction on the growth and development of large companies, therefore, necessarily affects the incentives and opportunities of small, nonpublic companies to invest and to reap the rewards of enterprise. In this connection, two aspects of smaller, nonpublic companies are discussed next: (1) entrepreneurs and small business persons who start or develop a business and for whom personal considerations are important; and (2) businesses that find mergers the most rational and preferable means of expanding or operating.

**Entrepreneurs and Small Business Persons.** Personal considerations that affect entrepreneurs and their families dominate the motivations of smaller, nonpublic companies toward merger with larger (usually public) companies. These factors are very important because they represent the opportunity for entrepreneurs to reap the rewards of their industry, their risk-taking, and their luck. Those who start companies or who take over and develop faltering companies often incur considerable personal sacrifice. Most such ventures fail; some succeed in varying degrees. If such an entrepreneur is not permitted to offer his or her company to the best among alternative buyers (this would include the management style of the acquiring company and its plans for the entrepreneur's employees and enterprise), the entrepreneur's expected rewards are reduced and the incentive to form new business enterprises is threatened. Moreover, for these small businesses the cost of raising capital by means other than merger will increase as investors anticipate a reduced possibility of realizing the rewards of success, or of "bailout" if the company falters. The result is damaging not only to the entrepreneurs but also to society as a whole. The nation will forgo the products, services, and jobs that potential

20

entrepreneurs would have provided had they not been handicapped by the merger ban.

Two additional basic reasons make the prospect of selling their companies via merger very important to small entrepreneurs. These reasons are (1) the need to diversify one's wealth and to obtain a liquid market for one's assets; and (2) the need to solve financial problems that limit the company's growth or threaten its survival. Mergers often (though not always) represent the most effective solution to these concerns.

*Diversification and liquidity.* Any entrepreneur is well advised to consider holding a diversified portfolio of assets. (In other words, "Don't put all your eggs in one basket.") In developing new businesses, however, entrepreneurs forgo this diversification, their "eggs" consisting not only of their capital but of their talents and energy as well. Once the individual businesses have achieved a size and stability that makes them attractive to others, entrepreneurs have the opportunity to diversify their investments by merging with a larger enterprise whose shares are publicly traded. This permits entrepreneurs to hold assets (shares) that can be readily sold. There are several important reasons why entrepreneurs will desire such liquidity.

One major purpose is the payment of income taxes. If dividends are distributed, relatively high income taxes must be paid. One way of reducing some of these taxes is to engage in a tax-free merger (exchange of shares) with a publicly traded company and then sell the shares as desired, paying taxes at capital-gains rates. Those who argue that this is not a socially defensible purpose, even though the tax reduction is permitted by law and is generally practiced, should recognize that it offsets somewhat the fact that our tax code is not symmetrical. It prohibits entrepreneurs whose businesses fail from deducting the whole of their losses as tax write-offs and from selling these write-offs to a profitable corporation through merger.[1] Furthermore, capital losses are deductible against capital gains or against other income in the amount (now) of $3,000 per year. Thus, the expected gain from success balances somewhat the expected loss from failure. In any event, as long as the tax laws are as they are, their effect as a motivation for mergers should be recognized.

---

[1] The Internal Revenue Code expressly prohibits an acquiring corporation from securing the benefit of a loss suffered by the acquired corporation if the principal purpose for such an acquisition was to secure the benefit of that loss. See Internal Revenue Code § 269. Other provisions of the code further limit the ability of entrepreneurs to transfer their unused tax losses through merger or acquisition. See §§ 382, 383, of the code.

Small business persons who do not plan for the means by which their estates can pay inheritance taxes risk both the continued viability of their enterprises and the financial security of their heirs. It is often difficult to sell a business with little notice, particularly if the founder dies unexpectedly. The result of unexpected death is thus often likely to be dissolution and losses to the heirs, workers, and society in general. This situation can be avoided by a merger with another company, after which some of the shares received can be used to pay the estate taxes. The alternative of exempting these estates from taxation is not desirable if one is concerned with the concentration of wealth. Large corporations into which successful smaller corporations often merge are usually owned by individuals less wealthy than the owners of private companies. Hence, tax exemption of inheritance of a business would benefit a wealthy class of individuals.

A second major reason why entrepreneurs may want to trade ownership of their own company for the shares of a larger, publicly traded company is to obtain access to the stock market as a source of funds for investment in other enterprises, of seed money for starting new businesses, of enjoyment of leisure time, and of the means for other expenditures for personal satisfaction. These are the opportunities and rewards of successful enterprise.

*Growth and survival.* Those who successfully start and develop small businesses often do not have the skills for or interest in developing the enterprises through subsequent phases of growth and change. They may lack the ability or the desire to manage larger enterprises or to develop new products, or they may want to reduce their own activities but may have no one available to take over. They may also want to raise capital for expansion, but (as is discussed below) a public issue of shares or debt is often more expensive than a merger. A merger also could be the least expensive route to expansion when it enables the smaller (or larger) enterprise to exploit a product quickly so as to avoid losing economic rents as competitors copy the product or develop alternatives.[2]

A merger with a larger enterprise can provide the skills and resources needed to preserve the smaller firm and solve its problems. As an example, consider the following acquisition reported in a recent issue of *Mergers and Acquisitions* (mergers of small, nonpublic companies are rarely described):

---

[2] This point was made by Julian Franks, who discusses it further in his dissertation in progress (London Graduate School of Business Studies).

For years, Green Giant had been floundering about with a sub-par return on investment and erratic earnings record. Pillsbury came up with an offer that couldn't be refused . . . a substantial premium over market. . . . Pillsbury's rationale behind the transaction was to gain Green Giant's strong position in frozen foods. This is an area of exceptional growth, but Green Giant's financial limitations had dictated against introducing and promoting new frozen food products. Now, with a fresh injection of capital from Pillsbury, there is every reason to believe that Green Giant can increase its market penetration in both canned and frozen foods.[3]

If merger possibilities are reduced by legislation, many of these enterprises may not survive at all. New ones would be deterred because of the perceived difficulties of realizing gains.

**Small Businesses for Which Mergers Are the Means of Raising Capital.** Many small businesses find the cost of raising capital in the public market very expensive. The costs of meeting the requirements of the Securities and Exchange Commission (SEC) are high. These include legal, accounting, and underwriting fees, all of which have increased. Since most of these costs do not vary much regardless of how much capital is raised, the costs per dollar of capital even for medium-sized companies can be considerable. For example, in 1971–1972 the direct cost of a public issue of common stock averaged 21 percent for an issue under $1 million, 7 percent for an issue of from $5 million to $10 million, and 3 percent for an issue of from $100 million to $500 million.[4] (Data for other years are similar.) In addition, as has been discussed, the stock market price of the average firm is currently below both its book value and its replacement cost. This situation is said by brokers to further increase the difficulty which smaller firms face in raising capital.[5] I believe that these factors explain the decrease in the number and dollar amount of new stock issues, particularly issues of

---

[3] "Mergers on Parade," *Mergers and Acquisitions* 14 (Summer 1979): 65. Similar descriptions may be found in this issue and other issues of this publication.

[4] U.S. Securities and Exchange Commission, *Costs of Flotation of Registered Issue, 1971–1972*, December 1974, p. 9.

[5] The SEC is attempting to alleviate this situation somewhat. On April 3, 1979, it announced an experimental program of simplified forms for public offerings for cash that do not exceed $5 million, in recognition of the present difficulties faced by small enterprises in raising capital (Securities Act Release No. 6049; Exchange Act Release No. 15691). In September 1979 the commission approved a proposed rule that allows companies to sell up to $2 million of securities in a six-month period without registration to institutions, to an unlimited number of persons who invest at least $100,000, and to no more than thirty-five other investors (*CPA Newsletter*, September 24, 1979, p. 8).

smaller companies. In this connection it has been reported that the number of new offerings decreased from 1,026 companies that raised $2,650 million in 1969 to 46 companies that raised $250 million in 1978.[6]

Merger with a larger company is, therefore, a cost-effective means by which many small enterprises can raise funds for expansion or survival. If such mergers are prohibited by legislation, the efficient flow of capital to productive small enterprises will be impeded, and many small businesses will find it difficult to raise the funds they require to modernize and grow.

It is important to note that constraints on mergers by *any* size class of companies affect entrepreneurs negatively. This constraint is equivalent to removing a group of customers for their product (their companies). This of course will reduce the returns they can expect to obtain for their enterprise. Not only may merger with what is actually the best partner be foreclosed, but the search and transaction costs of finding the best permissible merger partner are also increased. Resources will thus be used inefficiently because some "best" corporate combinations are foreclosed and, again, incentives for entrepreneurs initially to invest their energy and other assets are reduced.

While public stock issues are very costly to entrepreneurs, the raising of capital by merger is not. Since entrepreneurs (and their associates) control their corporations, they can refuse a proffered merger if they believe that it is disadvantageous.

A larger business is not inherently superior to a smaller one. If it were, the smaller enterprise could not have succeeded to the point at which it would be a desirable merger partner. Nor does the claim implied in this argument, that the greater amount of resources owned by the larger enterprise permits it to sustain more losses than its smaller rival (the "deep pocket" theory), have much validity (as is discussed in the next section). In any event, the anticompetitive use of a "deep pocket" is already prohibited by law.

In addition, data on new company formations support the conclusion that mergers (or the presence of large corporations) do not foreclose opportunities for new enterprises. *The Statistical Abstract of the United States* reports that net business formations and the number of businesses have been increasing both during periods characterized by mergers and during those not characterized by mergers.[7] As table

---

[6] *Wall Street Journal*, March 27, 1979.

[7] U.S. Bureau of the Census, *Statistical Abstract of the United States*, 1978, Table 914, p. 561.

# TABLE 1

## Growth in Net New Business Formations

A. Net Business Formations Relative to 1967 and New Incorporations, Selected Years

| Year | Relative Number of Net Business Formations (1967 = 100) | Number of New Incorporations |
|------|------|------|
| 1950 | 93 | 93,000 |
| 1955 | 99 | 140,000 |
| 1960 | 92 | 183,000 |
| 1965 | 99 | 204,000 |
| 1970 | 108 | 264,000 |
| 1975 | 109 | 326,000 |
| 1976 | 118 | 376,000 |
| 1977 | 127 | 436,000 |

B. Annual Growth Rates over Five-Year Periods by Types of Businesses (in percentages)

| Business Types | 1961–65 | 1966–70 | 1971–75 |
|------|------|------|------|
| Proprietorships | −0.03 | 0.70 | 2.97 |
| Partnerships | −0.58 | 0.48 | 2.77 |
| Corporations | 4.53 | 3.18 | 3.98 |
| All businesses | 0.43 | 1.00 | 3.10 |

Source: U.S. Bureau of the Census, *Statistical Abstract of the United States*, 1978, Table 914, p. 561.

1 shows, the conglomerate merger period that reached a crest in the late 1960s saw an increase in business formations over previous years. Over the following years the number rose even further, particularly in 1976 and 1977, years of the current so-called merger wave. The average five-year growth rates provide a further illustration. Over the years 1951–1970 new business formation grew by 4 percent a year, and over the years 1973–1977 by 8 percent a year.

Data on the total population of proprietorships, partnerships, and corporations show an even greater degree of small business health. As table 1, section B, shows, annual growth rates over the high merger periods saw increases rather than decreases in the number of new enterprises. It is difficult to see, therefore, how mergers have harmed entrepreneurs and other business persons in general.

Having examined these specific considerations with respect to smaller companies, I shall discuss the motivations for and consequences of mergers generally with respect to small and large companies alike.

## The Motivations for and Consequences of Merger Activity from the Standpoint of Shareholders

A merger is a joining of companies or a sale and purchase of assets. In the first case, stock is exchanged and the companies are "put together." In the second, one group of shareholders sells its shares and the other makes an investment. Shareholders benefit if the pooling or sale and investment give rise to greater values than would have been achieved if some other alternative had been followed. The nature of these benefits and of some alternatives is explored in this section. The possible bases for predicting benefits include: (1) potential for realizing monopoly profits; (2) economies; (3) diversification; (4) acquisition or sale of talents or resources not otherwise obtainable or salable; (5) superiority of mergers as investment opportunities; and (6) displacement of poor managers.

**Monopoly Profits.** An expectation of realizing monopoly profits, while theoretically conceivable as an explanation for merger activity, cannot realistically be viewed as a significant factor in light of the fact that section 7 of the Clayton Act broadly prohibits any actual or potential anticompetitive merger. The act has been applied so stringently that it has been used to bar procompetitive mergers.

While section 7 has most frequently been applied to horizontal and vertical mergers, it also bars conglomerate mergers if potential anticompetitive effects can be shown to follow. Conglomerates are infrequently banned under section 7 because the various anticompetitive motivations for or anticompetitive consequences of conglomerate mergers which have been asserted—(1) reciprocity, (2) reductions of potential competition, (3) predatory pricing and "deep pocket" behavior, and (4) mutual forbearance—are highly unlikely to occur in most situations. There is a considerable professional literature on these subjects.[8] Almost all of it demonstrates that these asserted anticompetitive effects of conglomerate mergers have almost no foundation in

---

[8] See Jules Backman, "Conglomerate Mergers and Competition," *St. John's Law Review* 44 (Spring 1970, Special Edition): 90–132, for an excellent discussion of the issue and review of the evidence. Many references to other works are given in this article.

either logic or evidence. Therefore, only a brief discussion of these issues is presented here.

*Reciprocity.* In his definitive article, James M. Ferguson defines reciprocity as "the bilateral practice in which the buyer agrees to purchase from the seller and the seller agrees to purchase from the buyer at specified prices."[9] The antitrust division of the Justice Department has successfully argued in the courts that reciprocal dealing restricts competition, particularly because it is a form of tie-in sale. Since conglomerates operate in many markets, critics have claimed that they have many opportunities for reciprocity and, therefore, conglomerate mergers are potentially anticompetitive.[10] This argument, however, is incorrect. As Ferguson shows, it has no foundation in economic theory. Where a firm has market power, it can use this power directly. Reciprocal buying arrangements cannot enhance this power.[11] Ferguson supports this conclusion with an analysis of several antitrust cases.

More important, however, is the likelihood that reciprocity is a means of evading anticompetitive price floors that are imposed by government regulations or private cartel agreements, or a means of reducing selling costs. A corporation that is forced to quote a price higher than the competitive price for its product (as when the Interstate Commerce Commission set a price below which a railroad could not charge) can offer price reductions to a customer by purchasing that customer's products at a higher than market price. This is what railroads did in offering to buy supplies from potential customers if they would ship their goods on the railroad that made the offer. Thus, the practice of reciprocal buying makes secret price-fixing agreements difficult to police, since the price cuts show up as higher costs of goods

---

[9] James M. Ferguson, "Tying Arrangements and Reciprocity: An Economic Analysis," *Law and Contemporary Problems: Symposium on The Antitrust Laws and Single-Firm Conduct* 30 (Summer 1965): 567.

[10] References to the documents in which these and other claims are made are given in Backman, "Conglomerate Mergers."

[11] In any event, the argument that conglomerates are particularly prone to reciprocal practices is inconsistent with the available evidence. Jesse W. Markham, in *Conglomerate Enterprise and Public Policy* (Boston: Harvard University, Graduate School of Business Administration, Division of Research, 1973), conducted a comprehensive study of the organization of conglomerates. His study of 211 corporations revealed that, if reciprocity is more likely to occur when a company maintains a trade relations department, it "is less likely to be practiced by highly diversified than by other corporations" (p. 80). In addition, the FTC's in-depth study of nine major conglomerates found that only 4 percent of the purchasing functions of acquired firms were changed after their acquisitions. See Stanley E. Boyle and Philip W. Jaynes, *Conglomerate Merger Performance: An Empirical Analysis of Nine Corporations* (Washington, D.C.: Federal Trade Commission, 1972), pp. 49, 55–56.

purchased rather than as lower sales and invoice amounts. Reciprocal buying and selling agreements can also reduce selling costs when they are used simply to formalize arrangements that reduce the need for sales efforts.

*Potential competition.* Potential competition is said to act as a constraint or limit on noncompetitive pricing, since market participants must consider the possibility that a potential competitor will enter the market. The difficulty with this argument is that potential competitors are not easily identified, since they are almost everywhere. Substitutes for most goods abound. For example, although only a few U.S. manufacturers make cars, actual and potential substitutes for new cars of U.S. manufacture include foreign cars, recreational vehicles, used cars, car repairs, and public transportation. These substitutes serve as competition to Ford, Chrysler, and General Motors.

It is well established that the potential competition doctrine has importance (if at all) only where the market in question is already dominated by a company with monopoly power. As Fritz Machlup stated in 1952, "Only if the single seller has a substantial share of the market will it pay him to forgo present profits to diminish the attractiveness of his trade to possible newcomers and thus maintain his 'control.' "[12] (I stress again here that situations of market dominance do not result from conglomerate mergers, since these mergers do not increase the corporation's share of any one market.) It is necessary to preserve a potential competitor only if potential competitors are *very* few and the market in which the firm is a potential competitor is monopolized. If it is competitive, or if potential competitors are many, no purpose is served by keeping a firm in its "potentiality" position.

The argument that a conglomerate merger may eliminate a potential competitor is also questionable because it assumes that, if a company did not enter a market via an acquisition, it would enter de novo. This reasoning is suspect because the costs of de novo entry, particularly in stable markets, often exceed the expected benefits (which, in fact, explains much merger activity). For example, a company may have developed a new product or process whose economically effective exploitation requires quick access to a market. By the time the company develops de novo facilities its competitors are likely to have learned of the product or process and to have acted to develop copies or substitutes. Alternatively, a company's competitors may have developed a new product that makes the company's product line less

---

[12] Fritz Machlup, *The Economics of Sellers' Competition* (Baltimore, Md.: Johns Hopkins University Press, 1952), pp. 110–111.

valuable to customers. The "damage" could be repaired only by means of acquiring additional facilities quickly, as via a merger or acquisition with another company that produces a similar product.

Moreover, the relative costs of de novo entry versus toe-hold acquisition are known to the firms already in the market; if the potential competitor does not try to buy in, these firms are unlikely to fear a more expensive de novo attempt to build in. Finally, the acquisition of an existing firm by another *is* the entrance of a different and, therefore, new competitor—and an actual competitor is likely to affect market behavior more positively than a potential one, particularly in concentrated markets.

*Predatory pricing.* The possibilities for predatory pricing are said to be enhanced by conglomerates and large companies because they have "deep pockets" and can afford to subsidize losing ventures with the profits from successful ventures. As is the case with the potential competition doctrine, a number of court decisions have banned vertical or conglomerate mergers on these grounds.[13] Below-cost pricing is itself unlawful under the antitrust laws;[14] thus, again, the anticompetitive effect feared is already covered by existing law. But, in addition, as has been demonstrated in many articles, the "deep pocket" argument assumes irrational behavior on the part of business persons.[15]

Predatory pricing is not a profitable way of competing, since the present value of the costs of driving one's competitors out of business is almost always greater than the present value of the monopoly profits one hopes to gain as a consequence. The major problem that the predator must face is how to prevent others (or the former com-

---

[13] See United States v. Falstaff Brewing Corp., 410 U.S. 526 (1973); FTC v. Procter & Gamble, 386 U.S. 568 (1967); United States v. Penn-Olin Chemical Co., 378 U.S. 158 (1964); General Foods Corp. v. FTC, 386 F.2d 936 (3rd Cir. 1967), cert. denied, 391 U.S. 919 (1968).

[14] See, for example, Janich Bros., Inc. v. American Distilling Co., 570 F.2d 848 (9th Cir. 1978), cert. denied, 47 U.S.L.W. 3195 (U.S. Oct. 3, 1978); Pacific Eng. & Prod. Co. of Nev. v. Kerr-McGee Corp., 551 F.2d 790 (10th Cir.), cert. denied, 434 U.S. 879 (1977); International Air Industries, Inc. v. American Excelsior Co., 517 F.2d 714 (5th Cir. 1975), cert. denied, 424 U.S. 943 (1976).

[15] See, for example, David R. Kamerschen, "Predatory Pricing, Vertical Integration and Market Foreclosure: The Case of Ready Mix Concrete in Memphis," *Industrial Organization Review* 2 (1974): 144, for a summary of a number of articles, and Donald E. Turner, "Conglomerate Mergers and Section 7 of the Clayton Act," *Harvard Law Review* 78 (May 1965): 1346, who concludes: "To sum up, predatory pricing seems so improbable a consequence of conglomerate acquisitions that it deserves little weight in formulating antimerger rules based on prospective effects."

petitors) from entering (or reentering) the market once monopoly has been achieved. This problem is likely to be even greater for conglomerates, since they rarely control a sizable share of any market.[16]

In other words, the mere fact that one can absorb losses longer before going bankrupt is no reason for wishing to do so. In any event, there is even less reason to expect this sort of illogical behavior from large corporations, whose managements are subject to various reviews and controls, than from the owner-managers of small corporations, who are less constrained from indulging in noneconomic behavior.

One other aspect of the "deep-pocket" concern should be considered explicitly—the claim that conglomerates and other large corporations tend to merge with or purchase dominant firms in a market, after which the "giants" use their considerable resources to further concentrate the market. The available evidence is totally inconsistent with this claim. The Federal Trade Commission's study of nine very large conglomerates found that "the conglomerates' positions in their product classes corresponded very closely in level of concentration to the average for all manufacturing."[17] The study also drew the following conclusion: "Thus, it does not appear on the basis of the 1969 product classes that conglomerates have followed a policy of making acquisitions in highly concentrated industries. . . . If anything, they have avoided or have been unable to buy into such industries."[18] The study goes on to state, however, that while conglomerates have not been devils, neither have they been angels: "Therefore, it seems unlikely that they have used their power to improve [decrease] concentration."[19] These conclusions are corroborated in a large-scale statistical study by Lawrence G. Goldberg of forty-four conglomerate mergers (most of which occurred in the 1960s) in fifteen different industries. He analyzed the changes in concentration after the mergers were effected and drew the following conclusion:

> Conglomerate mergers do not have a large effect on concentration. Companies acquired in conglomerate mergers do not grow significantly faster than other companies. Acquisitions by larger companies are not more likely to accelerate the growth of acquired companies. The best explanatory factor

---

[16] The FTC study of nine major conglomerates found that "in 81 percent of their product classes, the conglomerates have market shares of less than 5 percent" (Boyle and Jaynes, *Conglomerate Merger Performance*, p. 107). In addition, the study did not find any significant post-acquisition change in market shares.

[17] Ibid., p. 114.

[18] Ibid., pp. 114, 116.

[19] Ibid., p. 116.

of acquired firm growth which has been found is the pre-merger growth behavior of the acquired company.[20]

*Mutual forbearance.* It has been asserted by Corwin D. Edwards[21] and others that because conglomerates sell goods in a large number of common markets, they will recognize the usefulness of forbearing from active competition and, thus, tacitly will collude by adopting a policy of "live and let live." A feasible strategy of this nature, however, would require a great deal of centralized decision making, which is contrary to the organization of most conglomerates. Furthermore, it would require that the conglomerates be relatively large competitors in several of the affected markets; otherwise, a mutual reduction in competitive behavior would serve only to benefit the other (not mutually forbearing) firms. The Federal Trade Commission's study, however, stated: "It is apparent that the diversification of the survey conglomerates has been characterized more by breadth than depth. Most of their market positions are small and in only a few instances of their product classes can they be considered among the top firms."[22] In any event, since the positions of these conglomerates are not equal in all markets, balancing the gains from forbearance in one market against the losses in another would be an impossibly difficult task. In addition, if any trade-restraining collusion were detected, existing antitrust law would cover the situation.

In sum, aside from the fact that present law covers any potentially anticompetitive conglomerate merger, I must conclude that none of the four possible anticompetitive motivations for or consequences of conglomerate mergers is supported by economic reasoning or empirical evidence. Indeed, the logic and available data are contrary to the reciprocity, reduction in potential competition, predatory pricing and "deep-pocket" behavior, and mutual forbearance possibilities alleged.

**Economies.** The achievement of economies is a major expected beneficial consequence of, and is therefore a motivation for, mergers. These economies include the following:

- Joint production that takes advantage of scale economies and the greater range of products that can be produced jointly and commonly

---

[20] Lawrence G. Goldberg, "The Effect of Conglomerate Mergers on Competition," *Journal of Law and Economics* 16 (April 1973): 157.

[21] Corwin D. Edwards, "The Changing Dimensions of Business Power," *St. John's Law Review* 44 (Spring 1970, Special Edition): 416–438.

[22] Boyle and Jaynes, *Conglomerate Merger Performance*, p. 110.

- Integrated facilities that reduce transportation costs and supply uncertainty, and provide better monitoring and coordination of activities, etc.
- More efficient distribution, including integrated sales forces, wider product line, joint warehousing and shipping, and common advertising
- Economies in research and development
- Better use of management and other personnel, including exploitation of unused talents, greater opportunities for matching people and jobs, and economies in training and personnel management
- Lower costs of financing because of economies of scale in floating stock and bond issues and in obtaining bank loans
- Lower administration costs, particularly those imposed by governmental regulatory agencies and acts such as ERISA, EPA, and OSHA

Synergism is the term that includes all the above effects and means the benefit derived from putting two organizations together. Whether economies are achieved as expected is a difficult matter to measure. Against such economies, one has to consider the costs of mergers due to the integration of personnel, facilities, procedures, and computer programs, to take some examples.

No doubt there have been and will be instances in which it is clear after the fact that a merger was a mistake. But it should be even clearer that, to prevent people from making mistakes, government would have to prevent people from making decisions. Thus, good as well as bad decisions would be foreclosed. There seems little doubt that the record of business mergers shows overwhelmingly that most have been beneficial to shareholders, employees, communities, and consumers. (The evidence from which this conclusion is drawn is presented below and in chapter 3.)

Where mistakes have been made, divestitures have frequently been undertaken. Indeed, some conglomerates have been as active in selling off divisions that they found they could not manage as they have been in undertaking acquisitions. An indication of the extent of this activity may be garnered from a regular feature of *Mergers and Acquisitions* (a quarterly publication; 1979 is its fourteenth year of publication) entitled "Corporate Sell-Off." This feature briefly describes corporate divestitures of divisions and subsidiaries. For example, in the spring 1979 issue the first four of seventy-seven divestitures not previously reported included the following:

Gillette is selling its Welcome Wagon International subsidiary to its employees. . . . Pioneer Food Industries sold its steel canning division to Allen Canning for an undisclosed price. Esterline divested its subsidiary, Radioear, to an undisclosed company at a loss. Betz Laboratories sold most of the assets of two instrument-making subsidiaries, Uniloc and Kay-Ray, to Emerson Electric for an undisclosed consideration.[23]

The summer 1979 issue lists the "sell-offs" by types of purchasers. The purchasers and the numbers of recipients of divested firms are as follows: individuals, twenty-six; construction companies, two; manufacturing companies, forty-four; communications companies, six; wholesale trade companies, four; retail trade companies, six; financial operators, two; service companies, four; and agricultural products companies, one.[24]

**Diversification.** Mergers usually put together enterprises whose net cash flows over time are less than perfectly correlated. After a merger the cash flows generated by each of the formerly separate companies are added together, which dampens the magnitude of earnings peaks and valleys. Hence, merger can reduce the expected variance of these cash flows and thus reduce the risk that total cash flow will be negative, that bills will be unpaid, and that bankruptcy will have to be declared.

Contemporary finance teaches that shareholders can personally achieve a similar reduction in risk by holding a diversified portfolio of securities (such as mutual fund shares). However, shareholders still would bear the real costs of bankruptcy—such as legal fees, court costs, and inefficiently used corporate resources—which would be incurred should any of their companies go through dissolution. And the companies they own would have to pay higher wages if the companies were subject to a greater risk of bankruptcy. Whether or not shareholders hold diversified portfolios, therefore, they would still suffer if their companies could not diversify.[25]

---

[23] "Corporate Sell-Off," *Mergers and Acquisitions* 14 (Spring 1979): 34–36. This and the following issues were examined solely because they were the only ones readily available in the library. Companies described as "looking for a buyer," and similar indications of only possible divestitures, are not included in the seventy-seven.

[24] Ibid., pp. 48–51. William Sheperd reports that "selling off of branches rose in 1975 to 54 percent of all acquisitions (by number), up from 11 percent in 1967 and 39 percent in 1973" in *The Economics of Industrial Organization* (Englewood Cliffs, N.J.: Prentice-Hall, Inc., 1979), p. 163.

[25] For a rigorous treatment of the relationship between corporate diversification and risk that considers the benefits and costs to various classes of claimants, see

**Acquisition or Sale of Talents or Resources Not Otherwise Available or Salable.** In many instances the most efficient way for a company to obtain a work force, a research group, retail outlets, production facilities, and other such resources is to purchase an entire company. The alternative of building from scratch is often much more costly both to the company and to society. For example, a company may possess underused managerial talents, plant, distribution systems, or other resources that can be used more efficiently together with another company than through the creation of new facilities. And, as is discussed above, acquisition of existing facilities may be necessary to avoid delay in bringing a new or improved product or process to market.

As has been pointed out, the best price a company can get for its shareholders' investment is often obtained through a sale or merger of the company rather than through continued independent operations, and an acquisition is often the best investment that an acquiring company's management can make for the shareholders. These simple statements lie behind the operation of trading and markets. If the market for companies is constrained (as is proposed by suggested antimerger legislation), selling companies will not be able to get the best price for their shareholders and companies that are barred from making acquisitions will make less beneficial investments. As is the case with markets generally when they are thus restrained, resources are misallocated, and society is the loser. This elementary fact is at the heart of our antitrust laws.

**Displacement of Poor Managers.** At least since Adolph A. Berle and Gardiner C. Means published their book on the separation of ownership and control,[26] people have expressed concern for the possibility that managers might operate companies poorly or in ways contrary to the interests of the shareholders, but might not be replaced. Unlike sole proprietors or partners, shareholders of companies in which holdings are diffuse do not find it worth the costs of organizing to displace poor managers. In part, the market for managerial services—and, in particular, the pressures from lower managers whose positions and reputations are affected by the performance of their superiors—compensates

Li Way Lee, "Co-Insurance and Conglomerate Mergers," *Journal of Finance* 32 (December 1977): 1527–1537. Also see E. Han Kim and John J. McConnell, "Corporate Merger and the Co-Insurance of Corporate Debt," *Journal of Finance* 32 (May 1977): 349–365, for an empirical test that shows that stockholders do not lose to bondholders as a consequence of reduced cash flow variance that results from a merger.

[26] A. A. Berle, Jr. and Gardiner C. Means, *The Modern Corporation and Private Property* (New York: Macmillan, 1932).

for this and works to rid companies of poor managers. Managers at other companies compete for the jobs of poor managers and lower-ranked managers in their own companies work to remove them.

Poor managers can also be removed through the purchase of stock by a group that can gain control of enough shares to oust these managers. Except in the case of relatively small companies, the only investors with sufficient resources to gain control are other companies that make tender offers or conduct proxy contests. The rewards are the gains accruing from the removal of poor managers (that is, more productive and profitable use of company assets), which are expected to more than offset the cost of conducting the tender or proxy fight. Society also gains from more efficient use of resources and more efficient operation of companies by managers who fear that they would, in turn, be ousted by a takeover if they operated their companies badly.

Recent legislation such as the Williams Act and state laws that make "unfriendly" takeovers difficult and costly have blunted this tool for achieving the efficient operation of diffusely owned corporations. This legislation has protected existing managements. The argument made for these laws is that they allow all shareholders to receive a fair price for their shares. The claim is also made that the laws are necessary to permit management to inform shareholders of how well management has done its job. Unfriendly takeovers are also said to be destructive to the displaced managers and disruptive to communities. Whether there is sufficient merit to these arguments to offset the benefits from displacing poor managers, it seems clear that the legal balance currently is weighted against displacement. If anything, those who are concerned with the negative effects of the separation of ownership and control should recognize that the market for corporate control (as Henry G. Manne put it)[27] has become severely constrained by governmental regulation. Therefore, it would seem that those concerned should oppose any further constraints such as a limitation on a major group of participants in the market for companies.

### Empirical Evidence on the Effects of Merger Activity from the Standpoint of Shareholders

Despite the clear positive implications of merger activities from the standpoint of shareholders—of both the acquiring and acquired companies—it has been claimed (by Samuel Richardson Reid, among

[27] Henry G. Manne, "Mergers and the Market for Corporate Control," *Journal of Political Economy* 73 (April 1965): 110–120.

others)[28] that mergers are costly to these shareholders because the major motivating factor is rewards to managements that, on balance, are paid by shareholders.

A large number of empirical studies have been conducted that attempt to measure the benefits and costs of mergers to shareholders.[29] The studies can be divided into two groups: (1) those that use accounting-based measures of performance, and (2) those that use data based on the stock market.

**Accounting Data Studies.** The accounting-based studies suffer from several shortcomings that tend to invalidate their findings. One major shortcoming is the fact that accounting data often reflect economic values very poorly. This is a problem particularly for rates of return on assets or equity. Assets are measured at their original costs less an essentially arbitrarily determined periodic write-off (depreciation). The amounts are not adjusted for changes in price level. Intangible assets, such as the remaining economic value of advertising, research and development, employee training, managerial and production systems, and customer goodwill, are not recorded as assets. Shareholders' equity (book value) is affected also by accounting measurements of long-term debt that have not changed even though market interest rates have, and by divergences of accounting from economic net income. Net income is affected by accounting conventions—such as last-in, first-out (LIFO) or first-in, first-out (FIFO) inventory valuation, unrecorded changes in price levels, and expensing rather than capitalizing expenditures on research and development and other intangible assets—and by the inability of accountants to record assets and liabilities at their present values. The application of these conventions differs among companies and their effects differ in various periods. Furthermore, the numbers reported in accounting statements do not measure differences in risk among companies and over time.

Another shortcoming is that different degrees of leverage (the ratio of debt to equity) affect the levels of returns measured. Hence, a higher or lower profit amount or rate on assets or equity between merging and nonmerging companies, before and after a merger, cannot be ascribed unambiguously to the merger.

In addition, changing conditions not related to a merger affect

---

[28] Samuel Richardson Reid, *Mergers, Managers and the Economy* (New York: McGraw-Hill, 1968).

[29] Many of these studies are summarized by Dennis C. Mueller, "The Effects of Conglomerate Mergers," *Journal of Banking and Finance* 1 (December 1977): 315–347.

company performance. For example, Robert L. Conn compared the rates of return before and after merger on the assets of twenty-eight firms acquired during 1964–1968 by four major conglomerates, using data published by a House of Representatives 1971 staff report.[30] John F. Winslow, who previously reported these data to show that the postmerger profit rates of the acquired firms declined, concluded that the conglomerates were poorly managed.[31] Conn compared the returns on assets with returns to firms in similar industries and to the manufacturing sector over the same time period and found that "declining conditions in the industries of acquired firms and the manufacturing sector account for the poor performance of the acquired firms, not ineffective management."[32]

Thus, comparisons among companies or between the premerger and postmerger performance of a company rarely yield valid conclusions when they are based on the companies' accounting-determined net incomes or returns on assets or equity.[33]

**Stock Market Data Studies.** Stock market data are determined by market transactions that reflect directly the values of the assets exchanged. Since these assets are claims on companies, stock market prices provide direct and valid measurements of the economic values of companies. For this reason, many researchers have attempted to measure the effect of mergers by examining the changes in share prices of the affected companies.

Such measurements, however, pose two problems. First, the time at which investors first learned of the merger must be established. Second, the effects of factors other than the merger must be taken into account. These problems are simplified by the findings of a very large body of research, which show that the stock market is efficient. That is, share prices reflect in an unbiased manner (which is just as likely to include a positive as a negative error) the economic effect of all publicly available information at or very shortly after the time information becomes available. Therefore, changes in the share prices of the affected companies at or in a short period before and after a merger is

---

[30] Robert L. Conn, "Acquired Firm Performance after Conglomerate Merger," *Southern Economic Journal* 45 (Summer 1976): 1170–1173.

[31] John F. Winslow, *Conglomerates Unlimited: The Failure of Regulation* (Bloomington: Indiana University Press, 1973).

[32] Conn, "Acquired Firm Performance," p. 1172.

[33] See Mueller, "The Effects of Conglomerate Mergers," for citations to many of these studies. They are not further reviewed here because of their basic shortcomings.

*announced* provide a valid measure of the benefits or costs of the merger as valued by the companies' shareholders and other investors.[34]

A number of the published studies that use stock market data do not present valid results because they fail to overcome the two problems noted above.[35] Some of the studies take the returns to shareholders over the years following a merger, sometimes comparing them to the returns from some alternative investments, as measures of the profitability of the mergers. But they fail to account for other events that have affected the companies' share prices. Furthermore, they do not adjust the data for differences in risk among the companies compared. Because of these basic flaws the studies are not reviewed here.

Several studies do provide valid findings. They all use a variant of the "market model," which accounts for the effect on share prices of contemporaneous changes in conditions that generally affect the stock market.

*Methodology.* In brief, the market model measures the return $(R_{jt})$ to a common stock in company $j$ in period $t$ with the following equation:

$$R_{jt} = \alpha_j + \beta_j R_{mt} + \epsilon_{jt} \tag{1}$$

where $R_{jt}$ is the rate of return on stock $j$ in period $t$, measured as $(P_{jt} + D_{jt})/P_{jt-1}$ where $P$ is the market price adjusted for capital changes and $D$ is cash dividends paid; $R_{mt}$ is the rate of return on the portfolio of all the stocks traded in the market, measured as is $R_{jt}$; $\beta_j$ (beta) is a measure of the systematic risk of the stock, the relative variance of its returns with the market portfolio, and is measured as cov $(R_{jt}, R_{mt})$ / var $R_{mt}$; $\alpha_j$ is the portion of the stock's return not explained by the market and is often measured as $r_f (1 - \beta_j)$ where $r_f$ is the return on the risk-free asset or on any asset whose returns are uncorrelated with those of the market portfolio; and $\epsilon_{jt}$ is the residual (or disturbance term), which, in the absence of an unusual event, such as a merger or tender offer, is expected to have a value of 0 (zero).

This model enables the researcher to separate the effects of an event, such as a merger, which should be reflected in the residuals ($\epsilon_{jt}$),

---

[34] The objection of at least one researcher to this conclusion should be noted. Mueller (in ibid., p. 331) states that since a study of share prices "measures performance only *up to the date* of the merger, it is really a study of the market's *expected* gains from a merger, not the actual gains" (emphasis in original). Many studies have shown, however, that the market's expectations are unbiased (though possibly incorrect). Therefore, the share price data up to the date of the merger (if not before) do provide valid estimates of the benefits or costs of mergers to stockholders; these are the present value of the gains or losses to them.

[35] See ibid. for a review of and citations to these studies.

from the returns due to events that affect the market in general ($\beta_j R_{mt}$) and the expected returns to the normal operations of the company and the risk-free rate ($\alpha_j$), if we assume that the merger does not affect systematic risk ($\beta_j$).

The usual procedure is to aggregate into portfolios all the companies that engaged in mergers or tender offers over a fairly long period. This is done for two reasons. First, a large sample can be obtained. (For example, Peter Dodd and Richard Ruback used data from 344 companies over the period 1958 through 1976.)[36] Second, the effects of extraneous events, particularly those that occurred at the same time as a particular merger, are likely to be averaged out. For this purpose the researchers aggregate rates of return on the shares of companies engaged in a merger or tender offer into portfolios. For each company they define the time at which the public was informed about the event, usually by way of a public announcement, as period 0 (zero), whatever the actual calendar month (or week, etc.) in which it occurred. Thus, time 0 could be March 1959 for one company and June 1965 for another, for example.

The residual rates of return ($\epsilon_{jt}$), which are expected to capture the investors' assessment of the present value of the merger or tender offer, are estimated with the market model presented in equation (1). The $\alpha_j$ and $\beta_j$ are calculated with the use of data from periods before those believed to have been affected by a contemplated merger or tender offer.[37] Then these parameters are "plugged into" equation (1) to get the residuals ($\epsilon_{jt}$), with the use of data from the months before and after the date of the merger or tender offer announcement (period 0). The residuals are then averaged over the affected stocks (average residuals) and cumulated (summed algebraically) over time (cumulative average residuals). Some studies include statistical tests that indicate the probability that the average or cumulative average residuals are different from zero (that the merger or tender offer has benefited or hurt investors).

*Results.* The studies that have used variants of the methodology described, and hence present meaningful measures of the effect of mergers or tender offers on investors' wealth, include the following: Halpern, Mandelker, Langetieg, Asquith, Dodd and Ruback, and

---

[36] Peter Dodd and Richard Ruback, "Tender Offers and Stockholder Returns: An Empirical Analysis," *Journal of Financial Economics* 5 (December 1977): 351–373.

[37] A fairly complex methodology is employed to obtain stable estimates of the $\alpha_j$ and $\beta_j$ that meet the required statistical properties. The procedures are described in the studies.

Kummer and Hoffmeister.[38] The first four deal with mergers and the other two with tender offers. The merger results are discussed first.

Paul J. Halpern estimated the returns to shareholders of 155 companies that merged during the period 1950–1965. All of the companies were listed on the New York Stock Exchange (NYSE); all of the mergers were accomplished by exchanges of common stock for common stock or for assets. (Companies that engaged in repeated merger activity were not included.) Halpern classified the companies as "large" and "small" rather than as "acquiring" and "acquired." (This makes sense because exchange of shares and, in fact, the nature of merger makes "acquiring" and "acquired" ambiguous.) He found that the shareholders of both groups of companies gained, on the average, from their merger. The dollar amounts (adjusted for contemporaneous market and industry changes) were about equally divided between the two groups: the mean gain was $14.7 million to the shareholders of the larger companies and $12.6 million to the shareholders of the smaller companies.[39] In relation to the size of the companies, the mean adjusted gains expressed as premiums were 6 percent over the price of the larger companies' shares and 30 percent over the price of the smaller companies' shares. A nonparametric test on the sign of the returns indicated that the gains for both groups were significantly greater than zero.

Gershon Mandelker analyzed 241 mergers of NYSE-listed companies over the period 1941–1962 (91 percent of these occurred after January 1951). He found that the shareholders of the 241 acquiring companies earned only normal returns from mergers; the abnormal returns (adjusted for the market) are positive but not significantly different from zero. But the shareholders of the 252 acquired companies earned statistically significant abnormal returns that averaged 14 percent over the seven months prior to the merger (which period probably includes the date of the merger announcement). These results appear to be due to prior information about the merger that was available to

[38] Paul J. Halpern, "Empirical Estimates of the Amount and Distribution of Gains to Companies in Mergers," *Journal of Business* 46 (October 1973): 554–575; Gershon Mandelker, "Risk and Return: The Case of Merging Firms," *Journal of Financial Analysis* 1 (December 1974): 303–335; Terence C. Langetieg, "An Application of a Three-Factor Performance Index to Measure Stockholder Gains from Merger," *Journal of Financial Economics* 6 (December 1978): 365–383; Paul Asquith, "Mergers and the Market for Acquisitions," unpublished paper, University of Chicago, January 1979; Dodd and Ruback, "Tender Offers and Stockholder Returns"; and Donald R. Kummer and J. Ronald Hoffmeister, "Valuation Consequences of Cash Tender Offers," *Journal of Finance* 33 (May 1978): 505–516.

[39] The returns were considerably greater when they were not adjusted.

the market. Over the previous period (thirty-eight to nine months before merger) abnormal returns on the acquired companies' shares were negative. (This finding does not appear to be statistically significant.) After merger, the returns to shareholders of the combined corporations were found to be normal.

Terence C. Langetieg reexamined a subset (149 mergers) of the data used by Mandelker with a number of more complex and precise models, including a procedure that provided a matched sample of companies that did not merge. He found that the more complicated procedures yielded results similar to those reported by Mandelker, except that, with some models, the postmerger abnormal performance of the combined firms appeared to be significantly negative. However, when the paired-firm procedure was employed, this performance was seen as not significant. Thus, the poor postmerger performance of the consolidated companies appears to be due to factors at the time that affected similar companies similarly—factors that were not connected to the mergers. Langetieg draws the following conclusion:

> The acquiring firm exhibited an average excess return that from the most optimistic perspective was only 6.11%. The acquired firm fared somewhat better with an average excess return of 12.9%. These positive pre-merger [and apparently merger determined] excess returns indicate that the merger contributed to stockholder welfare. However, the gain is clearly too small to conclude that enhancement of stockholder welfare is the sole motive for merger. While the merger's impact is consistent with the hypothesis that the manager acts to maximize stockholder welfare, the small stockholder gain also suggests that perhaps another motive, such as managerial welfare, may have also been an instrumental cause of the merger.[40]

Considering that the average gains Langetieg reports are net of the present value of merger-related expenses, I do not understand why he concludes that "the gain is clearly too small. . . ."

Finally, Paul Asquith measured the gains or losses to shareholders of 305 acquired companies and 286 acquiring companies listed on the NYSE that were involved in mergers over the period 1946–1976 (fifteen railroad mergers were excluded). He found that shareholders of the acquired companies experienced abnormal losses averaging 14

---

[40] Langetieg, "An Application of a Three-Factor Performance Index," pp. 380–381. Note, however, that Halpern, in "Empirical Estimates," found a similar percentage (16 percent) to be worth $14.7 million, on the average, to the shareholders of the larger firms.

percent over the period from forty-seven to three months before the *announcement* of the merger. The average loss of 9 percent over the period from twenty-three to three months before the merger announcement is statistically significant.[41] From two months before the announcement through the announcement month, shareholders of the acquired firms gained abnormal returns averaging 14 percent, eight percentage points of which were realized in the announcement month. Shareholders of the acquiring firms obtained abnormal returns averaging 11 percent over the two years before the month of the merger announcement; about this, Asquith says: "These results suggest that firms do not actively seek acquisitions unless they [the acquiring firms] are doing well."[42] In the announcement month the acquiring companies' abnormal returns increase, but not by much. The twelve months' postmerger performance of the shares is not significantly different from normal.

Peter Dodd and Richard Ruback, in their study of tender offers, analyzed the returns to shareholders of 172 pairs of bidding and target companies (the shareholders of which were given tender offers) listed on the NYSE over the period 1956–1974. Their research is particularly noteworthy because they analyzed successful and unsuccessful tender offers (where the target companies were or were not taken over). They found that the shareholders of both groups of target companies earned large, statistically significant abnormal returns in the month of the announcement of the offer, averaging 21 percent for the successful offers and 19 percent for the unsuccessful offers. Furthermore, the share prices of the companies for which unsuccessful offers were tendered did not decline significantly thereafter. The shareholders of the successful bidding firms earned statistically significant abnormal returns averaging 3 percent in the announcement month; the shareholders of the unsuccessful bidders earned normal returns.

Donald R. Kummer and J. Ronald Hoffmeister analyzed the stock market behavior of eighty-eight NYSE firms for whom cash tender offers were made during the period 1956–1974. They divided the sample into three groups: passive-successful targets (forty-four firms

---

[41] Asquith, "Mergers and the Market for Acquisitions," p. 20. It should be noted that Asquith's findings pertain to a portfolio of acquired firms. The premerger downward trend that he observed could be due to one-time declines in the stock prices of individual companies at different points in time over the premerger period. This interpretation is consistent with the efficient market theory (and a large body of empirical evidence) which states that the reduction in share prices that represents the present value of the expected cost of poor management is effected completely when information about the management becomes known.

[42] Ibid.

in which a successful takeover was not resisted), resist-unsuccessful targets (fifteen firms in which a takeover was resisted and was not successful), and resist-successful targets (six firms in which a resisted takeover nevertheless was successfully consummated). For the sample as a whole, the cumulative abnormal returns (residuals) were consistently negative (generally increasingly so) from twenty-four months to eight months before the tender offer announcement. Over this period the cumulative average abnormal loss amounted to 10 percent. (This amount is statistically significant.) The resist-successful target shareholders suffered statistically significant negative abnormal returns of 22 percent over the period from twenty-four to four months before the tender offer announcement. The passive-successful target shareholders also experienced negative, though not statistically significant, abnormal returns averaging 6 percent. Only the resist-unsuccessful group's shareholders did not have negative abnormal returns: these were not significantly different from normal.

In the three months before the tender offer announcement, each group's shareholders experienced statistically significant gains averaging from 5 to 7 percent. In the announcement month shareholders obtained statistically significant gains of 16 percent for the passive takeovers, 20 percent for the resisted but successful takeovers, and 20 percent for the resisted and unsuccessful takeovers. The bidding firms' shareholders also received abnormal gains in the takeover announcement month, averaging 5 percent, after having received abnormal gains totaling 9 percent over the previous eight months. The returns thereafter were normal.

From these and other results presented in their paper, Kummer and Hoffmeister make the following statement:

> We offer the following scenario as an explanation of the preceding observations. Bidding firms seek out target firms for take-over. The focus is on the purchase of the rights to manage the assets of the target firm. In order to obtain those rights a premium is paid to the target's existing shareholders. However, in spite of the premium paid the value of the expected cash stream increases. Evidently capital market participants believe that the purchases of the target's shares and the right to control the firm's assets will generate an increase in cash flows that exceeds the cash outlay required.[43]

*Implications of the studies.* The findings of the studies can be used to evaluate various hypotheses about the effects of mergers and

---

[43] Kummer and Hoffmeister, "Valuation Consequences of Cash Tender Offers," p. 514.

tender offers on shareholders and on the competitiveness of markets, and about the motivations of management. First, it seems clear that the shareholders of acquired companies (or those to whom tender offers were made) benefited, since they received considerable gains in the value of their stock, ranging from about 14 to 20 percent through the time of the merger or tender of shares. Even in those instances where the tender offers failed, the shareholders' shares were considerably more valuable as a consequence of the offer. These findings are consistent with the belief that a function of company acquisitions is the discovery and repricing of undervalued assets. (The revaluation might stem from newly recognized prospective gains when the assets are combined with and managed by another company.) Acquisitions, therefore, also benefit the acquired companies' workers and communities, and society in general through the more effective use of resources. If the acquisition had been illegal or too costly to effect, these benefits would not have occurred.

Second, certain of the findings support the belief that some of these companies were poorly managed. The findings of Langetieg, Asquith, and Kummer and Hoffmeister to the effect that shareholders of acquired companies received statistically significant negative abnormal returns prior to the news of the merger are consistent with this hypothesis. While the other researchers did not find this phenomenon, their studies are consistent with the hypothesis that investors recognized that the bid-for companies would be more valuable if they were taken over, either presently (when the bids were successful) or in the future, as a consequence of their identification as merger prospects.

The studies also suggest that the shareholders of the acquiring companies benefit. Some studies show them receiving statistically significant positive abnormal returns even though their companies have announced that they intend to pay a substantial premium over market price for the shares of another company. Other studies show them receiving normal returns. This latter finding may be due to the expectation of investors in acquisition-prone companies that the companies will engage in mergers (by definition). Consequently, investors have incorporated the value of expected mergers into the share prices of these companies, and thus the prices tend not to increase very much when the mergers are announced. (This explanation is consistent with the fact that the shares of acquiring firms show positive abnormal returns before the merger announcement.) In any event, if the managers had engaged in mergers that were contrary to the best interests of their shareholders, the postmerger announcement share prices of these companies should have decreased in relation to the market; they did not. The data, thus, are inconsistent with the claim that mergers are undertaken by managers at the expense of their shareholders.

## The Motivations for and Consequences of Merger Activity from the Standpoint of Managers

In diffusely owned companies the decision to undertake an acquisition and to accept or reject a merger proposal generally rests with management, subject to the approval of the board of directors and, ultimately, the concurrence of the shareholders. Therefore, many observers (such as Reid and Mueller)[44] believe that mergers are undertaken primarily to further the interests of managers. However, as at least Mueller notes, and as the empirical evidence discussed above shows, these actions by managers need not be contrary to the interests of shareholders. Indeed, had shareholders believed that the mergers would not benefit them, the share prices (adjusted for general market conditions) of the average acquiring company would have decreased significantly instead of increasing or remaining unchanged.

The most obvious, but perhaps the most important, managerial reason for mergers (acquiring and acquired) is discussed above—the expectation that economies and other corporate benefits of various kinds will be achieved. A primary managerial task is discovering investment opportunities and opportunities for improving operations (research, production, marketing, finance, for example), estimating the costs and benefits thereof, making the investments and other changes decided upon, and managing the outcomes effectively. A merger is only one of the many possibilities that managers may consider. There is no reason to expect managers to decide on mergers with less (or more) effectiveness or consideration of the interests of shareholders than that which they bring to other major investment decisions. While managers no doubt make mistakes with respect to some decisions, there is no reason to believe that an outside observer (such as a court or government agency) would do better, and there is every reason to believe that someone not on the scene is likely to do worse.

One reason for expecting managers to act in the interests of shareholders is the operation of the market for managerial services. There are many people competing for managerial jobs. People in the same company and in other companies may displace a manager, who in turn is a present or potential competitor for the jobs of managers

---

[44] Reid, *Mergers, Managers and the Economy*, and Mueller, "The Effects of Conglomerate Mergers."

of other companies. It also is in the best interests of managers themselves that the companies that employ them do well. Hence, managers inside and outside of a company monitor each other and provide additional incentives for the effective operation of these companies.[45]

In addition, a larger, more diversified company provides greater breadth of opportunity for managerial talents. These challenges permit the managers to use their skills and earn monetary and nonmonetary rewards commensurate with their abilities. A large, diversified company can also offer managers and other employees the opportunity to change jobs and residences without having to change companies and thus lose seniority, accumulated knowledge, and personal relationships. To the extent that diversification reduces the risk of curtailed output and even bankruptcy, mergers offer managers and other employees greater job security. Furthermore, to the extent that managers are unable to diversify their portfolios of personal investments (perhaps because of stock purchase plans), a more diversified company offers them less risk. All of these benefits reduce the amount of salary that otherwise would have to be offered. Hence, unless there are more than offsetting costs, shareholders also benefit from the gains to management.

It is alleged, however, that managers who seek to effectuate or block mergers may act contrary to the interests of their shareholders. The managers of acquiring companies, it is alleged, seek growth for its own sake without regard to the economic desirability of a particular merger. Their motivation, it is argued, may be a desire to increase their salaries, to nurture their reputations as aggressive managers, or to enjoy the satisfaction of managing a larger enterprise.

If we assume for the moment that such motivations exist—at least for some managers—then we can say that there are two possibilities. One is that the managers may nevertheless make decisions that reflect the interests and risk preferences of their shareholders, as, for example, when the shareholders also believe that aggressive, growth-directed managers are more likely to achieve greater success, though perhaps through taking greater risks. The other possibility is that investors disagree with the managers' actions. In the former case the managers are serving their shareholders properly. In the latter case we would expect the companies' share prices to decline; initially, the shareholders lose, but the managers will also suffer, as they will find it increasingly difficult (expensive) to expand further by merger or by the raising of

---

[45] See Eugene Fama, *Agency Problems and the Theory of the Firm* Working Paper Series No. MERC 78-10 (Rochester, N.Y.: University of Rochester, November 1978) for a more complete description and analysis.

external capital. These managers will also become subject to displacement as a consequence of actions by the board of directors or takeovers by other companies—except, perhaps, when this self-correcting and disciplining mechanism is constrained by laws that restrict mergers or raise the cost of takeovers.

Other managers may suffer from the opposite limitation.. They may be overly conservative, nonexpansive, and unwilling to change. They may not be good at their jobs (or not as good as alternative managers). Nevertheless, they may be difficult to displace—in part because they possess considerable political, if not other managerial, skills or because they are allied with a dominant group of minority shareholders. In these (and similar) situations, the price of their companies' shares will decline and the companies will become vulnerable to takeovers. As is mentioned above, those concerned with managers who are not operating companies in the interests of their shareholders should want to encourage, rather than restrict, a free market for companies.

Nevertheless, let us consider the evidence of the apparent decrease in the prices of many large conglomerates' shares after the conglomerate merger wave of the late 1960s. Three possible explanations for this type of evidence should be distinguished. One is that the conglomerates' chief executive officers (CEOs) may have made the best decisions at the time for their shareholders by acquiring companies, but unpredictable subsequent events caused them to suffer losses. The second explanation is the possibility that the CEOs (and investors) honestly and in good faith overestimated the benefits to be derived from acquisitions. The third explanation is the possibility that the CEOs capriciously overestimated the benefits from mergers, realizing that they would gain if things turned out well and that only the investors would lose if the reverse occurred. The first two possibilities are merely possible outcomes of the decision-making process that is the strength of our economic system of free markets. Some decisions turn out well and some do not. A cost of making good decisions is the possibility that bad decisions will be made: to foreclose one is to foreclose the other. The last possibility, then, should reflect the essence of the critics' concern.

The validity of the possibility that the CEOs of large conglomerates acted capriciously against the interests of their shareholders can be tested empirically. Critics point to the fact that the conglomerates' senior officers' salaries continued at high levels even when the prices of their shares fell disastrously. Indeed, as Alfred Rappaport has described it, executives' bonuses often are determined by accounting-determined earnings, which may be greater as a consequence of acquisitions.[46] Salaries are only one part of the officers' economic rewards, however. They also hold shares and options on shares in the companies; therefore, should the share prices decrease (or increase) they share the costs (and rewards) with the other investors. The sum of the salaries, fringe benefits, and changes in the market value of investments in their companies measures the officers' economic compensation for their decisions. The question considered is whether the senior officers of conglomerates who had decision-making authority with respect to mergers had a personal economic stake in their decisions; in particular, did they benefit or lose along with their shareholders or did they benefit even when the shareholders lost?

These questions were answered with data gathered from the proxy statements of twenty-nine major conglomerates.[47] These conglomerates were chosen because they were included in an article by Malcolm I. Salter and Wolf A. Weinhold that was critical of conglomerate performance over the decade 1967 through 1977.[48] Officers who were also directors of their companies were considered to be those in decision-making authority. Their salaries (and estimated fringe benefits), stockholdings, and stock options for each year, 1970 through 1975, were obtained from the proxy statements. These were compared with the annual returns (stock price changes plus dividends per dollar invested) that the shareholders (and the officer-directors) experienced each year. These data (expressed in 1975 dollars) revealed salaries plus 20 percent for fringe benefits that averaged $174,000 annually. There was no relationship between the salary amounts taken alone and the returns on the companies' shares.

These returns varied considerably over the years studied. At one extreme, share prices declined by more than 30 percent for fourteen companies in 1970 and 1973 and for thirteen companies in 1974. At the other extreme, increases in share prices of more than 30 percent were experienced by ten companies in 1971 and twenty companies in 1975. The personal wealth of the officer-directors varied as well, since the dollar amounts of changes in the market prices of their shareholdings dominated their salaries. For example, the wealth (salary plus

---

[46] Alfred Rappaport, "Executive Incentive vs. Corporate Growth," *Harvard Business Review* 56 (July–August 1978): 81–88.

[47] For details see George J. Benston, "Conglomerate Managerial Motivations Towards Mergers: A Test of the Salary Maximization Hypothesis," unpublished paper (Rochester, N.Y.: University of Rochester, 1979).

[48] Malcolm I. Salter and Wolf A. Weinhold, "Diversification via Acquisition: Creating Value," *Harvard Business Review* 56 (July–August 1978): 166–176. The article lists thirty-six conglomerates; seven were omitted solely because complete data were not available.

change in wealth invested in shares) of the average officer-director of a conglomerate whose stockholders received a negative yield of 30 percent or less, declined (in 1975 dollars) by $1,328,000 in 1970, by $715,000 in 1971, and by $710,000 in 1974. The wealth of the average officer-director of a conglomerate, whose shareholders experienced a positive return of 30 percent or more, increased (in 1975 dollars) by $1,138,000 in 1971 and $1,735,000 in 1975. The results for the other years and levels of stock yields (adjusted and not adjusted for general market price changes) were similar. Furthermore, there was a positive association between the poor share price performance of a conglomerate and the termination of its officer-directors. Thus, these data show that the decisions made by the conglomerates' top managers affected these managers as much and as directly as they affected their shareholders; it is unlikely, therefore, that these officers acted capriciously in disregard of their shareholders' and their own interests.

## Merger Activity as a Function of the Interests of Merger Brokers

Another group that is said to benefit from mergers is merger brokers— the investment bankers, lawyers, and entrepreneurs who find prospects, perform analyses, give advice, and handle the paperwork. These specialists benefit, as does anyone else who performs a service. The only relevant question here, however, is whether, in some way, they cause mergers to occur that are not likely to benefit the shareholders of the companies.

There is little reason to believe that this concern is of any real importance. First, the considerable intertemporal increases and decreases in merger activity are inconsistent with the role of merger brokers as a major causal factor—unless it could be shown that the brokers' ability or desire to effect mergers has similarly ebbed and flowed. Second, managers, boards of directors, and shareholders need not take the advice of the brokers any more than they would take the advice of others who offer services to their enterprises. If they followed bad advice and damaged their companies through unsuccessful mergers, they would suffer directly. Third, merger brokers tend to be stable financial firms that depend on their reputations among investors, financial advisers, banks, and companies. Should they push mergers that tend to hurt investors, their reputations, and hence their fortunes, would suffer. Fourth, the studies reviewed above indicate that shareholders do not lose from mergers. Therefore, this possible causal factor seems to be of little, if any, importance.

# 3

# Consequences of Mergers to Society: Consumers, Workers, Communities, and the General Public

## Benefits and Costs to Consumers

Consumers benefit if production and distribution are conducted efficiently, since lower costs are reflected in lower prices, given the quantity and quality of output demanded. The resources saved by efficiency contribute to increased output and a higher standard of living.

As mergers are a means of adjusting modes of production and distribution to developing and changing circumstances, constraints placed on mergers are likely to be to the disadvantage of consumers. The efficient flow of capital to more productive areas of the economy would be impeded and economic growth and development would suffer. In addition, all of the benefits of enhanced economies and diversification discussed, with respect to shareholders, in chapter 2 would be lost to consumers as well if large conglomerate mergers were prohibited. Prices would be higher and product quality would decrease, since firms would be unable to pass on to consumers the economic gains they would have realized from mergers.

If mergers that reduce competition were consummated, there would, of course, be costs to consumers that might offset the benefits. Our antitrust laws, however, already prohibit this type of merger. There do not appear to be grounds for claiming that these laws are insufficient for this purpose. As the distinguished authority on antitrust laws, Richard A. Posner, testified before Senate Judiciary Committee hearings on S. 600 (the proposed antimerger act): "But I know of no responsible student of antitrust policy who believes that section 7 is too loosely drawn or interpreted or that a merger which seemed likely to reduce competition substantially on any plausible theory would be likely nonetheless to survive a challenge under section 7."[1] Similar views were expressed in the testimony of Ira Millstein,[2] past chairman of the American Bar Association's Antitrust Law Section, and Donald Baker,[3] former assistant attorney general in charge of the antitrust division.

Furthermore, the fact is that conglomerate mergers are more likely to increase rather than decrease competition. The acquisition by a conglomerate of a company in an industry new to the conglomerate is likely to add a new competitive force to the industry. Since, as the evidence on stock prices reviewed in chapter 2 shows, their acquisitions have, on the average, been doing poorly or are about to do poorly, the reinvigoration of the acquired company improves performance and service to buyers. While critics of conglomerate mergers have stated that a de novo entry into a market would be preferable to an acquisition of an existing firm, as discussed above, de novo entries are unlikely to occur or, when they do occur, to be viable.

On the basis of a survey of 193 companies that made 745 diversifying acquisitions over 1961–1970, Jesse W. Markham concludes that "while there are no means for determining the number of instances in which the acquiring firm would actually have entered through internal expansion had the acquisition route been foreclosed, it very likely would have occurred in fewer than 11 percent of the acquisitions."[4] Lawrence G. Goldberg and Stanley E. Boyle and Philip W. Jaynes, among others, also find that conglomerate mergers do not result in increased concentration.[5]

Therefore, all things considered, consumers would be net losers if firms above a certain size (or any firms) were prohibited from engaging in rational merger activity, so long as the resulting merger did not clearly create a monopoly or similar restraint of trade.

---

[1] Richard A. Posner, "Prepared Statement," in U.S. Congress, Senate, Subcommittee on Antitrust, Monopoly, and Business Rights, *Mergers and Economic Concentration: Hearings on S. 600*, 96th Congress, 1st session, April 26, 1979, p. 10.

[2] Ira M. Millstein, "Prepared Statement," in ibid., pp. 48–52.

[3] Donald I. Baker, "Prepared Statement," in ibid., pp. 34–44.

[4] Jesse W. Markham, *Conglomerate Enterprise and Public Policy* (Boston: Harvard University, Graduate School of Business Administration, Division of Research, 1973), p. 125.

[5] See Lawrence G. Goldberg, "The Effects of Conglomerate Mergers on Competition," *Journal of Law and Economics* 16 (April 1973): 137–158; and Stanley E. Boyle and Philip W. Jaynes, *Conglomerate Merger Performance: An Empirical Analysis of Nine Corporations* (Washington, D.C.: Federal Trade Commission, 1972).

## Benefits and Costs to Workers and Communities

Workers and the communities in which they work and live benefit or lose as employment opportunities expand or contract. The acquisition of a company by a conglomerate or other acquiring company may have either effect. However, it is more likely to have the effect of expanding employment—or of keeping it from contracting.

At this point it is important to clear up a misunderstanding on which opposition to conglomerate mergers has been based. Dennis C. Mueller, for example, makes the following statement:

> One cost of the pursuit of growth via external expansions, which has been cited in the literature, is that it is likely to come at the expense of more socially productive forms of growth [Reid and Sichel are cited]. *Mergers compete directly with capital investment, R&D and other investment-type expenditures for cash flows* and managerial decision-making capacities. While a manager is perhaps indifferent [as to] whether a given rate of expansion is achieved through internal or external growth, society is likely to be better off through the creation of additional assets. [Emphasis added.][6]

This statement contains two major fallacies. One is that a merger effected by an exchange of shares or bonds involves a use of assets other than for transactions costs. This type of merger does not compete for the available supply of capital with expenditures on new plants, or on research and development, for example. If anything, such a merger is likely to facilitate transfers of resources among units of the combined company to those uses where their net marginal values are the greatest. This type of transfer benefits the economy generally.

The second fallacy is the claim that the acquisition of a company for cash is a substitute for alternative investments which would be socially preferable. As is discussed above, the conglomerate or other acquiring company generally does not have better capital investment or research and development opportunities or it would not seek the acquisition. If it were required to use resources for these other activities, the resources would probably be wasted, to the detriment of the investors and of society. Furthermore, while it is true that if the conglomerate distributed the cash to its shareholders they could invest in other com-

---

[6] Dennis C. Mueller, "The Effects of Conglomerate Mergers," *Journal of Banking and Finance* 1 (1977): 339. The works cited are Reid, *Mergers, Managers, and the Economy*, and Werner Sichel, "Conglomerateness: Size and Monopoly Control," *St. John's Law Review* 44 (Spring 1970, Special Edition): 356–377. Sichel does not make this argument strongly.

panies, they would first have to pay income taxes on the dividends. And while it is possible that some of these funds would be invested in the companies that otherwise would have been acquired by the conglomerate, this possibility is doubtful—particularly for smaller, regional businesses because of their difficulties in raising equity capital. In any case, *there is no reason to believe that the distribution of cash to current shareholders of the company would result in greater investments in new plant and equipment than would the distribution of cash to the shareholders of an acquired company.*

The net effect of prohibiting conglomerate mergers, therefore, is more likely to be a decrease in growth and investment, with corresponding decreases in employment or in the rate of rise of productivity and wage rates. Workers and communities would suffer as new and improved job opportunities were lessened.

Restricting conglomerate mergers would also deprive employees and communities of the benefits of diversification. Since such diversification, as has been discussed previously, is often too costly to achieve through de novo entry, mergers are frequently the only rational means by which large and small companies can diversify their operations.

Diversification benefits employees by providing them with more opportunities for advancement, training, and locations in which to live, among other advantages. In effect, a larger, diversified company permits employees to change jobs without changing companies. Employees and communities also benefit from diversification because of the greater stability in output (due, in part, to the ability of a larger company to shift production among plants as demand changes) which such diversification can bring. A small, regional, single-industry firm is also more likely to go bankrupt than is a larger, diversified enterprise. This conclusion is based on the greater impact on the smaller, regional firm of local economic depressions, product demand declines, and technology changes. In addition, a larger, diversified company generally has greater access to capital funds at lower cost for changes and expansion of facilities.

Of course, some employees may prefer working for a smaller, locally owned company. And some local merchants may prefer dealing with owner-operators whom they have known for a long time. In addition, acquiring companies may discontinue products, close plants, or manage their new operations poorly. Critics of mergers claim that these activities are more characteristic of large, diversified companies than of smaller, regional companies. This claim appears to be based on two assumptions. As the following analysis shows, neither of them is persuasive.

One assumption is that small companies are likely to be operated by entrepreneurs or closely related groups of investors who may be involved in local community affairs and therefore may be more concerned about the welfare of the community But this paternalistic attitude can be dysfunctional: the concerned local business persons also may use their position and wealth to impose their personal tastes in aesthetics, morality, and power on their communities. In any event, there is no evidence that *in general* local firms would choose to maintain a plant that is not operating successfully.

The other assumption supporting the contention that smaller companies may be less likely to close down local plants is that smaller companies may be operated by people who have unusual talents or who are otherwise superior to the employees of larger companies. It may be that some talented managers prefer working for local companies, but there are others who prefer working for large, diversified companies. One would expect that the market for managerial services would operate much as other markets to equate the cost and availability of managerial services among firms. However, the large companies may have an advantage over local companies if the cost of moving within a company is less than the cost of moving among companies. In addition, the larger, diversified companies are more likely to achieve economies in operations and finance, for example, that permit them to operate a facility more efficiently.

Data from two very different sources support the conclusion that large, diversified companies are not more likely to be associated with plant closings. The first is derived from a special survey of establishments that went out of business during 1975 conducted by the Bureau of the Census of the U.S. Department of Commerce. The survey showed that 24,800 single-unit establishments employing 250,000 people in 1974 ceased operations, compared with 3,100 multiunit establishments employing 229,200 people. As percentages of the total numbers of establishments and their employees in existence in 1972 (the latest available year), 9.58 percent of the single-unit establishments with 5.25 percent of that group's employees went out of business, compared with 4.41 percent of the multiunit establishments with 1.61 percent of that group's employees.[7]

The second source is the closing of steel plants in Youngstown, Ohio, which has attracted attention as an example of the measure of

---

[7] U.S. Bureau of the Census, *1974–1975 Annual Survey of Manufacture*, Table 1. Establishments That Have Gone Out of Business During 1975 By Size Class; unpublished data; and U.S. Bureau of the Census, *Statistical Abstract of the United States*, 1978, Table 1407.

54

discretionary power by an absentee management. In 1969 the Youngstown Sheet and Tube Company merged with Lykes Corporation, which has its headquarters in New Orleans. In 1977 the Lykes Corporation closed the former Youngstown Sheet and Tube Campbell Works. In December 1977 Lykes and Ling-Temco-Vought (LTV) merged, when Attorney General Griffin Bell overruled the recommendation of his antitrust division. LTV (through its subsidiary, Jones & Laughlin, which absorbed the former Youngstown Sheet and Tube) announced that it would close a second Youngstown steel mill, the Brier Hill Works, at the end of 1979. Staughton Lynd is the lawyer for the Brier Hill union and the Ecumenical Coalition of Mahoning Valley (which includes the affected mills), a group formed to save the mills. In an article, he analyzed the charge that: "Lykes had milked a perfectly good steel company and then shut it down because of its own failure to modernize the equipment." Lynd wrote that this explanation

> was "inadequate." It assumed a division of the world into "good" steel companies which plow earnings back into technical improvements, in fact, and "bad" steel companies which divert earnings elsewhere, when, in the second half of 1977 practically all American steel companies were shutting down older facilities. Thus Bethlehem Steel laid off men in Lackawanna, New York, Armco Steel laid off men in Middletown, Ohio, and Wheeling-Pittsburgh Steel did the same. None of these companies was owned by a conglomerate. United States Steel, too, participated in what industry journals termed the "shakeout" by announcing that it would run its mills in Youngstown only so long as they were profitable without new investment. Thus the Number One company in the industry declared publicly that it was willing to do exactly what Lykes had done before the Campbell Works shutdown.[8]

As this close observer, who is not sympathetic to business in general or to conglomerates, recognizes, basic economic difficulties similarly affect the decisions of companies, whether these companies are large or small, or are conglomerates or not.

### Benefits and Costs to the General Public: Considerations of Centralized Business Power

Perhaps the principal concern of the supporters of legislation to foreclose mergers of large corporations is the centralization of wealth and

---

[8] Staughton Lynd, "The Fight To Save the Steel Mills," New York Review of Books, April 19, 1979, p. 37.

power. For example, the chairman of the Federal Trade Commission, Michael Pertschuk, stated that "unrestrained conglomeration could conceivably result in the concentration of an enormous aggregation of economic, social and political power in the hands of a small number of corporate leaders, responsible in a formal sense to stockholders but in a real sense only to themselves."[9] He emphasized this concern, stating:

> Indeed, it is almost impossible to ignore the fact that values beyond economic efficiency are important reasons for anti-trust enforcement. These other values seem to me to be fairly obvious. Foremost, probably, is the maintenance of a multiplicity of decision centers—opposition, that is, to undue aggregation of centralized economic, political or social power or authority. . . . This is not a trivial or academic concern; the political and social power held by executives of large conglomerate enterprises is significant.[10]

Similar statements were made by other government officials and private individuals who testified in favor of legislation proposed to limit mergers and the market for companies. Therefore, this concern merits further consideration. For that purpose, the use of the aggregate concentration ratio (ACR) as a measure of centralized business power is analyzed just below; this is followed by a brief discussion of other relevant aspects of the centralized business power issue.

**The Aggregate Concentration Ratio as a Measure of Centralized Business Power.** The ACR is the ratio of the assets, sales, value added, or profits of the largest 50, 100, or 200 corporations to a total for all corporations. Financial corporations are usually omitted from the numbers because a large part of their assets are claims against the assets of the nonfinancial corporations; hence, corporate resources would be double counted if the financial corporations were included. In recent years (since about 1964) the ACR has been presented for manufacturing corporations only.[11]

---

[9] Michael Pertschuk, "Prepared Statement," in U.S. Congress, Senate, Subcommittee on Antitrust and Monopoly, *Mergers and Industrial Concentration: Hearings on Acquisitions and Mergers by Conglomerates of Unrelated Businesses,* 95th Congress, 2nd session, May 12, July 27, July 28, and September 21, 1978, pp. 154–58.

[10] Ibid., p. 156.

[11] The history of the ACR and an excellent analysis of its meaning and shortcomings are given by David Schwartzman, "Prepared Statement," in Senate, Subcommittee on Antitrust, Monopoly, and Business Rights, *Mergers: Hearings on S. 600,* April 26, 1979. Much of the following discussion is drawn from his statement.

The ACR suffers from problems of two basic kinds, which almost completely invalidate it as a meaningful measure of economic concentration: (1) measurement problems and (2) conceptual problems. Each type is discussed briefly.[12]

*Measurement problems.* Two principal factors bias the ACR when it is applied to manufacturing corporations only. One is that the entire assets and sales of a corporation are included as manufacturing if at least 51 percent of these numbers are believed to be related to manufacturing, even though the balance represents nonmanufacturing activities (such as distribution, mining, financing, and services). The second is that the ACR is supposed to provide a measure of concentration in the U.S. market; nevertheless, it is contaminated and biased when the data include the foreign sales and assets of U.S. corporations. Until 1973 the foreign assets and sales of U.S. corporations were included in the data. Because the largest corporations, more than the smaller ones, have tended to diversify into nonmanufacturing and foreign operations, these errors bias the ratio upward, giving the unwary a misleading impression of increasing concentration. F. M. Scherer points out, for example, that the 46 percent share of manufacturing assets which the Federal Trade Commission says was held by the leading 100 companies in 1963 turns out to be 36 percent when foreign and nonmanufacturing assets are stripped from the data.[13] Furthermore, manufacturing is, relatively, a declining portion of gross national product, having dropped steadily from 29 percent in 1950 to 26 percent of the total in 1976. Hence, it is not useful to concentrate on this sector if one wants a measure of the concentration of economic power.

Even for the manufacturing sector, however, the ACR has been stable over time. For manufacturing corporations, FTC data cited by David Schwartzman show that the ratio of the assets held by the largest 100 manufacturing corporations to total manufacturing assets increased only from 46.4 percent in 1960 to 47.6 percent in 1972. With foreign assets removed, the ratio dropped to 44.7 percent in 1973 and stood at 45.5 percent in 1976. A similar pattern is shown for the largest 200 manufacturing corporations, which had 56.3 percent of all manufacturing assets in 1969, 60.0 percent in 1972, 56.9 percent in

---

[12] See ibid.; see also Betty Bock, "How Big Are the Biggest Companies? Aggregate Concentration: Concepts, Numbers, and Perceptions," and J. Fred Weston, "Prepared Statement," in ibid.

[13] F. M. Scherer, *Industrial Market Structure and Economic Performance* (Chicago: Rand McNally, 1971), p. 40.

## TABLE 2

### AGGREGATE CONCENTRATION RATIOS IN TERMS OF ASSETS OF NONFINANCIAL CORPORATIONS

(in percentages)

| Asset Group | 1958 | 1963 | 1967 | 1972 | 1975 |
|---|---|---|---|---|---|
| Top 50 | 24.4 | 24.4 | 24.5 | 23.4 | 23.3 |
| Top 100 | 32.1 | 31.7 | 32.0 | 30.7 | 30.6 |
| Top 150 | 37.4 | 36.7 | 37.3 | 35.9 | 35.6 |
| Top 200 | 41.1 | 40.5 | 41.2 | 39.9 | 39.5 |

SOURCE: Schwartzman, "Prepared Statement," in Senate, Subcommittee on Antitrust, Monopoly, and Business Rights, *Mergers: Hearings on S. 600*, Table 2, p. 600.

1973, and 58.0 percent in 1976.[14] (There is no way to determine whether these changes are due to chance, measurement errors, or trends of some sort.)

The less biased and more relevant numbers for nonfinancial corporations, similarly, show stability over time. The assets of the top 50, 100, 150, and 200 corporations, in relation to all nonfinancial corporate assets, were almost unchanged in five-year periods from 1958 through 1975, as table 2 shows.

But these numbers are also biased with respect to their stated meaning as a measurement of the change in aggregate corporate power. For this purpose, the degree to which the largest corporations as of a given time are increasing their share of total corporate assets, sales, etc., would seem appropriate. The data presented above give the shares of the largest corporations at a point in time, even though those in the top 50, 100, etc., at one year-end are not the same as those at the other year-ends. The more relevant numbers present the share of the same group of the largest corporations as of some particular date and at succeeding dates. These numbers indicate (to the extent that such numbers can) the changed share of the largest corporations over time. Table 3 shows these data for the largest 50 and 100 corporations in terms of value added by manufacture. Also shown are the shares of 1970's largest corporations traced backward to 1947. It seems clear that

---

[14] Schwartzman, "Prepared Statement," in Senate, Subcommittee on Antitrust, Monopoly, and Business Rights, *Mergers: Hearings on S. 600*, Table 1, p. 598.

## TABLE 3

SHARE OF TOTAL VALUE ADDED BY MANUFACTURING ACCOUNTED FOR
BY THE LARGEST MANUFACTURING CORPORATIONS: 1947 TO 1972

| Largest Corporations | Percent of Value Added by the Identical Largest Corporations in Each Year | | | | | | |
|---|---|---|---|---|---|---|---|
| | 1947 | 1954 | 1958 | 1962 | 1966 | 1970 | 1972[a] |
| In 1947 | | | | | | | |
| 50 largest | 17 | 21 | 20 | 21 | 21 | 19 | 17 |
| 100 largest | 23 | 27 | 27 | 27 | 27 | 26 | 24 |
| In 1970 | | | | | | | |
| 50 largest | 12 | 19 | 20 | 22 | 24 | 24 | 23 |
| 100 largest | 18 | 25 | 26 | 29 | 31 | 33 | 32 |

[a] The extension to 1972 (the latest available year) was provided to the author by Professor Weston.
SOURCE: Weston, "Prepared Statement," in Senate, Subcommittee on Antitrust, Monopoly, and Business Rights, *Mergers: Hearings on S. 600*, Table 7, p. 545.

the share of the same group of largest corporations[15] has declined over time. (It is also noteworthy that the share of the largest corporations in 1970 had declined by 1972.)

However, the shares of the corporations that are largest as of the end of a period (1970 in table 3) show considerable increases over time. The reason is obvious: if they had not grown they would not be in the top group. This is why they displace members of the original group that grew at lower rates. In fact, Betty Bock has calculated the following turnover rates between 1947 and 1977 of the membership in the top groups (in terms of assets) as follows: top 50, 42 percent; top 100, 39 percent; and top 200, 42 percent.[16] Such instability does not seem indicative of increasingly concentrated power in corporations (assuming that the ACR is a valid measure of power).

*Conceptual problems.* The conceptual problems to which the ACR is subject are even more significant than are the measurement problems and may be illustrated by identifying the specific "largest" companies and their industries that make up the numerator of the ratio. J. Fred Weston points out that 30 percent of total value added in the U.S. economy is provided by six industries: motor vehicles, chemicals, pe-

---

[15] Note that the only period over which the ACRs increased, 1947–1954, was a period of relatively little merger activity.
[16] Bock, "How Big Are the Biggest Companies?" in ibid., Table 3, p. 531.

troleum, steel, electrical products and equipment, and aerospace.[17] These six comprise only about 4 percent of the total number of U.S. industries. In addition, as table 4 shows, 35 of the top 50 *Fortune* companies are in these industries. Even a cursory knowledge of the six industries reveals that they are characterized by large-scale, capital-intensive manufacture, and that the economies from this scale are what determine their large size. It should be recognized, therefore, that a concern over the level of aggregate concentration is really a concern about the scale of manufacturing in certain industries. Unless one is willing to sacrifice the economies of scale—or buy shoes and walk rather than buy cars and drive—there is little that can be done to reduce the level of the ACR.[18]

The listing in table 4 of the fifty largest corporations illustrates further the lack of conceptual meaning of the ACR. The ratio purports to measure the degree of centralized business power. Yet the largest corporations are a group only in the sense that production and distribution technology dictate large scales of operation for the six industries delineated. There is little reason to expect firms from different industries to be a cohesive group that might pose a threat of centralized power.

Most significantly, the ACR has no relevance as a measure of the only meaningful type of economic power—concentrations of power within particular markets. Economic power is the ability to control prices and industry output and should not be confused with wealth or profitability. By definition, pure conglomerates do not enhance such power since the power of a monopolist to control price and output cannot be summed across different markets. The ACR is thus a meaningless tool with respect to the existence of economic power. I next consider the extent to which large diversified corporations have economic or political power as measured in other ways.

**The Elements and Extent of Corporate Power.** Edwin Epstein, an eminent scholar of the political power of business, summed up his assessment of the state of knowledge when he testified before the Senate Subcommittee on the Judiciary's hearing on a proposed antimerger act that, "there does not exist at this time a sufficiently reliable empirical base concerning the nature, extent and implications of corporate politi-

---

[17] Weston, "Prepared Statement," in ibid., p. 536.

[18] In this regard, it should be noted (as demonstrated in Weston's testimony) that the various "waves" of recent merger activity have in no way materially affected the level of aggregate concentration—if we assume that the level of this number has any meaning at all.

## TABLE 4

### Largest 50 Companies Listed in Fortune Magazine, Ranked by 1977 Sales

| Rank | Industry and Company | Rank | Industry and Company |
|------|----------------------|------|----------------------|
| | *Motor Vehicles* (4 companies) | | *Steel* (2 companies) |
| 1 | General Motors | 15 | U.S. Steel |
| 3 | Ford | 35 | Bethlehem Steel |
| 10 | Chrysler | | *Electrical Products, Computers* (6 companies) |
| 28 | International Harvester | | |
| | *Petroleum* (17 companies) | 7 | IBM |
| 2 | Exxon | 9 | General Electric |
| 4 | Mobil | 11 | ITT |
| 5 | Texaco | 18 | Western Electric |
| 6 | S.O. Calif. | 26 | Westinghouse |
| 8 | Gulf Oil | 30 | RCA |
| 12 | S.O. Ind. | | *Others* (15 companies) |
| 13 | Atlantic Richfield | 19 | Tenneaco |
| 14 | Shell Oil | 20 | Procter & Gamble |
| 17 | Continental Oil | 22 | Goodyear |
| 23 | Sun Oil | 29 | Eastman Kodak |
| 24 | Phillips | 32 | Caterpillar Tractor |
| 27 | Occidental Petroleum | 34 | United Technologies |
| 33 | Union Oil | 36 | Beatrice Foods |
| 42 | Ashland Oil | 27 | Esmark |
| 45 | Amarada Hess | 38 | Kraft |
| 47 | Cities Service | 39 | Xerox |
| 48 | Marathon Oil | 40 | General Foods |
| | *Chemicals* (4 companies) | 41 | R. J. Reynolds |
| 16 | DuPont | 43 | LTV |
| 21 | Union Carbide | 44 | Firestone Tires |
| 25 | Dow Chemical | 50 | 3M |
| 44 | Monsanto | | |
| | *Aerospace* (2 companies) | | |
| 31 | Rockwell | | |
| 49 | Boeing | | |

Source: Weston, "Prepared Statement," in Senate, Subcommittee on Antitrust, Monopoly, and Business Rights, *Mergers: Hearings on S. 600*, Table 2, p. 538.

cal and social power to permit Congress to formulate legislation with the requisite level of information and insight required for sound public policy."[19] I completely concur in this assessment and believe that any

[19] Edwin M. Epstein, "Prepared Statement," in ibid., April 26, 1979, p. 64.

conclusions drawn about the political power of large firms at this time would be premature. Nevertheless, considering the importance of this issue to those who favor legislation that would severely constrain or prohibit mergers, some comments are appropriate.

*Economic power.* It is important, first, to emphasize again that most corporations have very little economic power. (Economic power may be defined as the ability to control prices and industry output and should not be confused with wealth or profitability.) Most markets are very competitive, because there is a wide range of products and services that are substitutes for one another. For example, Campbell may be the only manufacturer of its branded soups, but it must compete with Heinz, Lipton, privately labeled soups, and all other types of foods and alternative products, including restaurant meals and home-made soups. General Motors may be the largest producer of automobiles, but consumers can purchase Fords, Plymouths, Gremlins, Volkswagens, Toyotas, or used cars. Or they can have their cars repaired, use public transportation, or engage in carpooling. DuPont may be the only manufacturer of a given chemical, but users can substitute alternatives that are almost as good or are better, depending on the prices of the alternatives and the changing production processes.

Thus, the power of managers over prices is severely constrained by the consumer's ability to use substitutes. Similarly, the managers' control over production is determined by consumer demand for the companies' products. The abilities of the companies to pay lower wages or lower prices for materials or any other factor of production are limited by the fact that workers and suppliers need not supply them with their services and products. They can go elsewhere when others offer better wages and prices. Although the managers have the discretion to keep an inefficient plant in operation or to raise wages above the market, they will lose money and eventually their jobs. Division managers must answer to the board of directors and to the shareholders; if a manager's poor performance is not corrected or if he or she is not removed, the corporation's share prices will decline and it may be taken over. Although a takeover may not occur, the threat of one is an incentive for managers to do their jobs well. If merger-restricting legislation beyond that already in existence is enacted, the effect of this incentive will be severely blunted. Thus, this type of legislation will enhance, not restrict, the power of corporate managers.[20]

The power of the chief executive officer (CEO) of a conglomerate

---

[20] The existing limits upon discretionary corporate power are further described by Millstein in his prepared statement in ibid., pp. 48–52.

to close the plants or move the headquarters staff of an acquired company has been mentioned as an argument for prohibiting or restraining mergers. Therefore it should be considered, if only briefly. It is important to note that the president (and/or board of directors) of *any* company has the authority and responsibility to make decisions of this type: someone must make the final decision. The CEO who makes poor decisions is punished by the marketplace, as is pointed out above. But it might seem that the CEO of a large conglomerate has more power than the CEO of a smaller, one-industry company.[21] Although this question has not been adequately researched, I believe that the decentralized organizational structure of most conglomerates in fact gives their presidents less discretionary power.[22] Plant closings and similar decisions are likely to be proposed by the relevant division vice-presidents, who act on the advice of their staffs and plant managers. Such a decision is reviewed at corporate headquarters and the CEO is often faced with a documented proposal that he or she can approve or disapprove if the question is close. But it is doubtful that the CEO has the sole power to initiate and determine a plant closing or similar action. In contrast, the president of a small company, particularly one owned by family interests, has this power, or at least has greater leeway than does the CEO of a decentralized conglomerate.

*Political power.* Political power may be defined as the ability to influence the passage of legislation and the administration of laws and regulations. That large corporations possess such power unduly is doubtful. Two aspects of political power are analyzed next: the effect of mergers on reducing the number of independent decision-making units, and the relative amount of political power between large and small companies.

Proponents of anti-conglomerate-merger legislation have voiced the concern that mergers result in fewer independent decision-making units. This concern is faulty in two essential respects—one factual and the other conceptual. Factually, conglomerate mergers have not reduced the number of decision-making business enterprises—certainly not.in particular markets, nor in the economy as a whole. As was discussed in chapter 2, the number of large and small business enterprises has increased substantially before, during, and after recent merger "waves."

---

[21] See the analysis of the steel plant closing in Youngstown, Ohio, presented above in Chapter 3.

[22] Markham's *Conglomerate Enterprise and Public Policy* and Boyle and Jaynes's *Conglomerate Merger Performance*, in-depth studies of conglomerate organizations, support these conclusions.

The conceptual fault is that a larger number of corporations per se is not a good measure of the degrees of business independence and weakness of political power. A very important limiter of power, competition, is often greater when the competitors are a few companies roughly equal in size than when there are many companies in a market. Moreover, as companies become more diversified, operating in different markets, they are more likely to reflect the broader interests of the general public rather than the narrow interests of firms with operations of limited scope.

In addition, although formal study is needed, a review of some observable data supports the conclusion that large, diversified corporations are likely to have *less* political power than smaller, specialized enterprises. Consider, for example, the trucking industry, the resident forms of which have benefited from a government-run cartel that sets prices and restricts entry. Yet the industry is characterized by many relatively small specialized firms. The maritime shipping industry provides a similar example. Milk producers and doctors are another. These industries comprise many companies and individuals that have been able to get federal and local governments to fix prices and restrict entry into their domains.

Another example is banking. While the industry has some large banks, most of the more than 13,000 banks are small. A review of the legislation that regulates the industry reveals the following restrictions on and biases against large banks.[23] Interstate branching is forbidden by the McFadden Act. Branching within many states is prohibited or restricted. Expansion of banks into other areas via holding companies is controlled by the Federal Reserve. Large banks, almost all of which are members of the Federal Reserve System, are taxed by being required to keep non-interest-bearing reserves; the reserves imposed by the states on the generally small nonmember banks can be met by holding certain income-yielding assets. Large banks tend to serve depositors with large balances; Federal Deposit Insurance Corporation insurance premiums are imposed on all deposits, even though balances up to only $40,000 are insured. Having extensively researched this area, I am able to say that most, if not all, of the politically determined regulations and laws favor the small banks over their large competitors.

These examples illustrate the general observation that smaller, specialized businesses have more political power than large, diversified

---

[23] See George J. Benston, "The Optimal Banking Structure: Theory and Evidence," *Journal of Bank Research* 3 (Winter 1973): 220–36, for an extensive analysis.

conglomerates have. This is the case, in part, because there are more small than large businesses. Although the chief executive officer of a single small company may have less "clout" than the CEO of a large conglomerate, there are many more small company CEOs. As a group they can be in contact with many more legislators, legislative aides, regulators, newspaper editors, and other politically important persons than can the CEOs of the large conglomerates. Furthermore, as Epstein points out, "of the 812 corporations which had registered political action committees [PACs] with the Federal Election Commission as of September 30, 1978, less than half (333, or 41 percent) were among the giants of American business as measured by inclusion on any of the 1978 *Fortune* lists of the 1,300 largest American companies in seven industry classifications."[24]

Aside from these numbers, it is clear that the statutory limitations on affiliated PACs of $5,000 per candidate per election necessarily reduces this form of influence by very large companies. As Epstein also notes, the maximum usefulness of "conducting political action by means of a Washington public affairs or governmental relations office most likely occurs at a size of firm substantially smaller than the giants which are the concern of these hearings."[25]

The possible political power of large conglomerates should also be compared with the political power of other organizations. While, again, a formal study is required, a few obvious examples can be mentioned—one being labor unions. It is doubtful that any corporate president has the political power of the late George Meany or Frank Fitzsimmons. Certainly, none has the longevity in office, command over resources that can be devoted to political ends, or ability to influence such large numbers of voters as these and many other labor leaders. A second example is the heads of government agencies. The several cabinet officers and numerous commissioners and administrators—all unelected and possessing enormous discretion—have authority over more resources and persons than do most—perhaps all—corporate CEOs.

Thus, although the data are insufficient for drawing reliable conclusions about the political power of corporations at this time, the data we do have tend to indicate that large companies do not wield disproportionately great political power.

---

[24] Epstein, "Prepared Statement," in Senate, Subcommittee on Antitrust, Monopoly, and Business Rights, *Mergers: Hearings on S. 600*, p. 67.

[25] Ibid., p. 69.

# 4
# Conclusion

Legislation has been proposed that would prohibit or severely curtail mergers beyond the present restrictions imposed by section 7 of the Clayton Act, as amended by the Celler-Kefauver Act in 1950 and as interpreted by the Supreme Court. The analysis presented above leads to the conclusion that this legislation is not desirable. Instead of benefiting, it would harm American entrepreneurs, shareholders, managers, workers, communities, and consumers, as well as our political democracy. Therefore, even if it cost nothing to administer it would be bad legislation. But the proposed legislation is unlikely to be costless to administer, and it is likely to have additional dysfunctional effects.

## The Costs of the Proposed Merger Prevention Legislation

Senate bill S.600 (somewhat ironically entitled the "Small and Independent Business Protection Act of 1979") is an example of the legislation that has been proposed. If it were enacted it would do the following:

1. Ban mergers between firms having annual sales or assets exceeding $2 billion.

2. Ban mergers between firms having annual sales or assets exceeding $350 million, unless the merger "will result in substantial efficiencies," or "within one year before or after the consummation of the transaction the parties shall have divested one or more viable business units the assets and revenues of which are equal to or greater than the assets and revenues of the smaller party to the transaction."

3. Ban an acquisition by a firm with assets or revenues exceeding $350 million of a firm that has "20 per centum or more of the net

sales during the calendar year immediately preceding the acquisition in any significant market," subject to the same defenses as described above in (2).

Supporters of the bill have claimed that it imposes a per se rule that will be easy to administer, since the rules are clear and the burden of proof for an exception rests with those who would merge. However, that assessment appears to be seriously in error.[1]

First, the essential terms that frame the rules are subject to varying interpretations. Assets can mean net or gross of depreciation, inclusive or exclusive of subsidiaries (domestic or foreign), inclusive or exclusive of the capitalized value of leased property, etc. Sales are also subject to alternative interpretations. For example, an insurance company's sales are not comparable to those of a manufacturer, but to the bill, they are the same. Perhaps most important, the definition of a market cannot be specified in advance. The Standard Industrial Code definitions are notoriously out of date. At best they refer to similarities in production rather than in demand. Moreover, it is not clear whether foreign companies are subject to the proposed act. If they are not, they clearly will gain a competitive advantage over U.S. companies in making acquisitions. If they are, the Justice Department will be faced with the diplomatically delicate task of imposing a severe set of regulations on foreigners.

Second, and of greater economic significance, the act invites avoidance by accounting and real economic actions. As William F. Baxter describes in greater detail,[2] a management whose corporation is near the $2 billion or $350 million dollar limits that wants to make itself merger-proof can juggle assets and sales. Assets can be inflated by reducing depreciation by use of a straight-line rather than an accelerated method (if net assets are the definition), using first-in, first-out accounting for inventories when prices are increasing, and owning rather than leasing assets, among other techniques. Sales can be inflated by including freight-out in the selling price. Costs to society in the form of wasted resources would be incurred if physical actions rather than bookkeeping entries were used to inflate the accounting numbers. For example, the corporation could purchase rather than rent assets such as warehouses, plant, and equipment; owned trucks could

---

[1] The following discussion is based in large measure on the statements prepared by Richard A. Posner, Donald I. Baker, and William F. Baxter in U.S. Congress, Senate, Subcommittee on Antitrust, Monopoly, and Business Rights, *Mergers and Economic Concentration: Hearings on S. 600*, 96th Congress, 1st session, April 26, 1979. See their statements for much more complete analyses.

[2] Baxter, ibid.

be used instead of public carriers; and products with high selling prices could be added to the line. Thus, poor managers not only would foreclose their displacement but would further waste corporate resources. As Baxter points out, the cost of these actions is likely to be great, since over 130 of the publicly held industrial firms listed by *Fortune* could cross the $350 million boundary with only a 10 percent alteration in their assets or sales.

Third, the defenses specified are in fact available only at considerable expense, if at all. It is very difficult to understand how anyone can demonstrate that a merger *will* substantially enhance competition. For example, how can one manager be shown to be a more effective competitor than another? Any claim that substantial economies *will* result is nearly impossible to establish. On one hand it is easy to claim that great economies will follow from a merger. But, on the other hand, with the many changes that occur even normally it is virtually impossible to prove the source of decreased or increased expenses. Hence, the authorities will have the burden either of believing or of disbelieving the parties. Their decision will probably be made even more difficult by the claims of those who want to block a merger (such as managers who would be replaced or competitors who want to preserve a merger prospect or foreclose additional competition).

Finally, the limits specified in the bill are not indexed for changes in the purchasing power of the dollar. Should inflation continue, an increasing number of corporations will be foreclosed from mergers. Posner has calculated the effect of this fault (assuming that it was not intended) on the mergers that took place from 1967 through 1976 among companies whose shares were listed on the New York Stock Exchange (NYSE).[3] On the assumption that the bill would not be indexed (that the limits in 1967 would have been half those in the present bill, since the price level has doubled since 1967), he calculates that 84 percent of the mergers among NYSE companies would have been foreclosed. But even had the bill's presently stated dollar limits been in force since 1946, roughly three-quarters of all NYSE company mergers would have been in jeopardy. This bill, therefore, presents the economy with a truly Draconian solution to a nonproblem.

## Alternative Remedies

The response one often encounters after demonstrating that a proposed action is much more likely to be damaging than helpful (even in terms

---

[3] Posner, ibid.

of the expressed values of the proposer) is, "Well, then, what do you propose for dealing with this situation?" This question presupposes that the situation is one that requires dealing with. The discussion presented above indicates, I believe, that current mergers do not represent a problem that needs remedying. For one thing, the current merger wave, if it be one, appears to be due to economic conditions that would not be remedied were mergers prohibited or restricted. Instead, the post-Clayton Act mergers (and certainly the post–Celler-Kefauver Amendment mergers) tend to facilitate the efficient allocation of resources in the economy and to be a means of rewarding entrepreneurs for the efforts and risks they undertook. If anything, there is reason to believe that the laws have been so strictly applied that they block business combinations that would be desirable for achieving a more efficient use of resources.

What, then, are the arguments that would support further restrictions on mergers? As an aid to ensuring that few, if any, important points made by proponents of antimerger legislation are omitted, the report of the attorney general on conglomerate mergers is considered briefly.[4] The letter submitting the report "to the President, and the Senate and House of Representatives of the United States in Congress assembled" states its authority, purpose, and conclusions, as follows:

> The Small Business Act . . . directs the Department of Justice to review the activities of Government for the purpose of determining "any factors which may tend to eliminate competition, create or strengthen monopolies, promote undue concentration of economic power, or otherwise injure small business." This report analyzes the competitive and social impact of mergers and acquisitions among and by our largest business enterprises, paying particular attention to the issues posed by conglomeration and to the ability of the antitrust agencies to deal adequately with conglomerate mergers under existing legislation. Generally, the report concludes that mergers among large enterprises, on balance, contribute little to economic efficiency, while enhancing the aggregate concentration of economic power and creating the potential for significant injury to small businesses. The report concludes, however, that the existing anti-merger provisions of the Clayton Act do not adequately deal with conglomerate mergers and recommends the enactment of legislation that

---

[4] John H. Shenefield, *Report of the Attorney General Pursuant to Section 10(c) of the Small Business Act, as Amended: Conglomerate Mergers, Small Business, and the Scope of Existing Anti-Merger Statutes* (Washington, D.C.: U.S. Department of Justice, June 20, 1979).

would prohibit certain types of mergers and acquisitions by the largest businesses unless they enhance competition.[5]

The thirteen statements that follow reflect all of the major (and some minor) arguments that are presented to support the recommendations for more antimerger legislation.[6] Each statement is followed by a brief analysis or reference to an analysis presented above. These analyses lead to rejection of all of the statements.

1. Current merger activity constitutes a wave that serves to reinforce the increasing concentration of economic power in the economy. This conclusion is based entirely on aggregate concentration ratio (ACR) data that I strongly believe are empirically incorrect and conceptually wrong in their application. (See chapter 3.)

2. "Conglomerate mergers by large firms have served to diminish the number of decision centers in the business community." As is discussed in chapter 3, neither data on the growth in the number of independent businesses nor the realities of decision making by large or small corporations support this assertion.

3. "On balance conglomerate mergers have few economic benefits for the companies involved." The studies of the stock market reaction to mergers (reviewed in chapter 2) reveal a totally contrary picture. Shareholders of acquired companies gained considerably while shareholders of acquiring companies either gained or did not lose. The studies cited by John H. Shenefield generally are not germane to the question because they do not (and given the methodology employed, cannot) separate merger-related events from other events, or are unsupported assertions of belief.

4. "The bulk of conglomerate acquisitions may involve well-managed firms. Rather than serving to stimulate managers to try to improve performance, fear of takeover, to the extent that it motivates management of potential targets, logically would act as a disincentive to corporate efficiency." If this argument were valid, legislation that encourages rather than prevents takeovers would be called for. The quoted assertion is followed by the statement that "the takeover phenomenon has produced negative side effects. Successful firms that fear they may become takeover targets have attempted to reduce their attractiveness by using accumulated cash to acquire other corporations in an effort to create antitrust conflicts with likely acquirers." This assertion also leads one to expect that the attorney general would op-

---

[5] Ibid., first page (unnumbered).

[6] The material that is directly quoted below is all from ibid., pp. 2–15.

pose rather than support antimerger legislation such as S.600, since (as discussed above) this bill would encourage additional wasteful merger-proofing actions.

5. The managerial and research advantages of conglomerates have been overstated by their proponents. Whether or not this is the case generally (although there are probably examples of it), it is not a valid argument for prohibiting or restricting the growth of conglomerates. This is a decision that investors should be permitted to make.

6. "Perhaps the most overt effect of mergers and acquisitions among America's largest businesses is the contribution they make toward the increasing concentration of power in relatively fewer and fewer corporations. . . . Large enterprises may have undue influence on the political officers of the nation." As is discussed in chapter 3, the conclusion on economic concentration is based on bad metrics (the ACRs). Furthermore, the number of independent business units has increased rather than decreased during periods characterized by mergers (see table 1). Since Shenefield's "political influence" conclusion is supported by reference to Charles Lindblom's critique of corporate enterprise, Lindblom's conclusion as to what should be done about these institutions should be of interest.[7] Lindblom closes his book with the following statements: "It is possible that the rise of the corporation has offset or more than offset the decline of class as an instrument of indoctrination. . . . More than class, the major specific institutional barrier to fuller democracy may therefore be the autonomy of the private corporation. . . . The large private corporation fits oddly into democratic theory and vision. Indeed, it does not fit."[8] He appears to be calling for the abolition of private corporations. Considering this conclusion and the often confusing (and confused), rarely documented analysis of this book, its citation by Shenefield as authoritative is surprising.

7. "Conglomerate mergers may direct corporate financial resources or loan capacity from investment in new productive facilities." This fallacy is discussed in chapter 3, and is dismissed, since the total resources of the nation are not diminished by mergers; indeed, if resources are used more efficiently, they are increased.

8. "As long as companies continue to have the opportunity to diversify through acquisition, including acquisition of relatively domi-

---

[7] Charles Lindblom, *Politics and Markets* (New York: Basic Books, 1977).

[8] Ibid., p. 356. Shenefield, *Report*, cites pages 344–56. The last line quoted is the last line of the book.

nant firms, they cannot be faulted for avoiding the more pro-competitive means of diversification, de novo entry or purchase of a firm with a relatively small market share." The arguments and data reviewed above (see particularly chapter 2) do not support the assumed facts, nor does it logically follow that the suggested activity would be undertaken because of merger restrictions or would be more pro-competitive.

9. "Conglomerate mergers facilitate the emergence of mutual forbearance on the part of major firms." This argument also is considered in chapter 2, and is rejected completely.

10. "The chief threat to small business rivals resulting from the acquisition of a competitor by a large enterprise is that the transaction will 'entrench' the competitor's market position or enable the acquired firm to 'invest' in short-run predatory conduct for the purpose of achieving the benefits of a dominant position thereafter." The "deep pocket" and "predatory pricing" arguments are discussed in chapter 2. There, as in most of the professional economics literature, they are dismissed as contrary to both logic and empirical studies.

11. Small business may be hurt by the conglomerates' ability to achieve economies in advertising, distribution, credit, and purchasing.[9] This argument contradicts statement 3, to the effect that conglomerates usually are not efficient forms of business organization. Moreover, small businesses are only hurt by the economies of large firms if the small firms are not allowed to merge with, or merge together to become, large firms.

12. "A conglomerate merger may decrease the commitment of an acquired firm to the financial and civil health of its local community." This assertion is considered in chapter 3, and is rejected.

13. "Larger enterprises . . . gain a substantial, if artificial, competitive advantage where regulation exists." This assertion is not supported by the available data, reviewed in chapter 3.

In short, the Justice Department bases its call for legislation that would restrict or prohibit conglomerate and other mergers on the grounds that not all mergers are successful and that large enterprise is "a bad thing." Few, if any, of its assertions are based on valid evidence. As I believe this study demonstrates, the department's reasoning is also faulty. Certainly, it does not support the conclusion that more antimerger legislation would be beneficial to the nation.

Finally, it may help to put the issue in focus to remember that mergers are an outcome of a competitive market for companies in which assets are freely traded, subject to overriding statutes such as

---

[9] Shenefield, *Report*, pp. 12–13.

section 7 of the Clayton Act. It would, I am sure, raise a serious antitrust question and probably violate the Sherman Act if large companies above, let us say, $350 million in sales or assets entered into an agreement that they would not purchase each other's shares. That kind of agreement is tantamount to an agreement not to compete and would restrain trade in assets. The proposed antimerger legislation would be, quite clearly, just as anticompetitive. It would restrain and unsettle the market for assets in general, making that market thinner and less liquid, and would create new costs which ultimately would be passed on to consumers in the form of higher product prices. We should require just as compelling a reason to interfere substantially in this market as we would require to pass a law which fixes or limits the amount of steel or number of automobiles that large companies may produce. In all of these cases, natural competitive forces would be constrained. While such government interference in the marketplace is not always unwise or unwarranted, no evidence or valid reasoning has been put forth that would support an imposition of such constraints on the market for corporations.

# BIBLIOGRAPHY

Arthur Andersen & Co. *Cost of Government Regulation Study for the Business Roundtable.* Chicago, Ill.: March 1979.

Asquith, Paul. "Mergers and the Market for Acquisitions." Unpublished paper, University of Chicago, January 1979.

Backman, Jules. "Conglomerate Mergers and Competition." *St. John's Law Review* 44 (Spring 1970, Special Edition): 90–132.

Benston, George J. "Conglomerate Managerial Motivations Towards Mergers: A Test of the Salary Maximization Hypothesis." Unpublished paper, University of Rochester, Rochester, N.Y., 1979.

―――. *Corporate Financial Disclosure in the UK and the USA.* London: Saxon House, D. C. Heath Ltd.; Lexington, Mass.: Lexington Books, D. C. Heath & Company, 1976.

―――. "The Optimal Banking Structure: Theory and Evidence." *Journal of Bank Research* 3 (Winter 1973): 220–236.

Berle, A. A., Jr., and Means, Gardiner C. *The Modern Corporation and Private Property.* New York: Macmillan, 1932.

Boyle, Stanley E., and Jaynes, Philip W. *Conglomerate Merger Performance: An Empirical Analysis of Nine Corporations.* Washington, D.C.: Federal Trade Commission, 1972.

Briloff, Abraham J. "Accounting Practices and the Merger Movement." *Notre Dame Lawyer* 45 (Summer 1970): 604–628.

"Conglomerate Mergers and Acquisitions: Opinion & Analysis," *St. John's Law Review* 44 (Spring 1970, Special Edition).

Conn, Robert L. "Acquired Firm Performance after Conglomerate Merger." *Southern Economic Journal* 43 (October 1976): 1170–1173.

Dodd, Peter, and Ruback, Richard. "Tender Offers and Stockholder Returns: An Empirical Analysis." *Journal of Financial Economics* 5 (December 1977): 351–373.

Edwards, Corwin D. "The Changing Dimensions of Business Power." *St. John's Law Review* 44 (Spring 1970, Special Edition): 416–438.

Eis, Carl. "The 1919–1930 Merger Movement in American Industry." *Journal of Law and Economics* 12 (October 1969): 267–296.

Fama, Eugene. *Agency Problems and the Theory of the Firm.* Working Paper Series No. MERC 78-10. Rochester, N.Y.: University of Rochester, November 1978.

Feldstein, Martin, and Summers, Lawrence. *Inflation and Taxation of Capital Income in the Corporate Sector.* Working Paper No. 312. Cambridge, Mass.: National Bureau of Economic Research, January 1979.

Ferguson, James M. "Tying Arrangements and Reciprocity: An Economic Analysis." *Law and Contemporary Problems: Symposium on the Antitrust Laws and Single-Firm Conduct* 30 (Summer 1965): 552–580.

Goldberg, Lawrence G. "The Effect of Conglomerate Mergers on Competition." *Journal of Law and Economics* 16 (April 1973): 137–158.

Gort, Michael. "An Economic Disturbance Theory of Mergers." *Quarterly Journal of Economics* 83 (November 1969): 624–642.

"The Great Alaskan Oil Freeze." *Business Week*, February 26, 1979: 74–88.

Halpern, Paul J. "Empirical Estimates of the Amount and Distribution of Gains to Companies in Mergers." *Journal of Business* 46 (October 1973): 554–575.

Hong, Hai; Kaplan, Robert S.; and Mandelker, Gershon. "Pooling vs. Purchase: The Effect of Accounting for Mergers on Stock Prices." *Accounting Review* 53 (January 1978): 31–47.

Kamerschen, David R. "Predatory Pricing, Vertical Integration and Market Foreclosure: The Case of Ready Mix Concrete in Memphis." *Industrial Organization Review* 2 (1974): 143–168.

Kim, E. Han, and McConnell, John J. "Corporate Merger and the Co-Insurance of Corporate Debt." *Journal of Finance* 32 (May 1977): 349–365.

Kummer, Donald R., and Hoffmeister, J. Ronald. "Valuation Consequences of Cash Tender Offers." *Journal of Finance* 33 (May 1978): 505–516.

Langetieg, Terence C. "An Application of a Three-Factor Performance Index to Measure Stockholder Gains from Merger." *Journal of Financial Economics* 6 (December 1978): 365–383.

Lee, Li Way. "Co-Insurance and Conglomerate Merger." *Journal of Finance* 32 (December 1977): 1527–1537.

Lindblom, Charles. *Politics and Markets.* New York: Basic Books, 1977.

Lynd, Staughton. "The Fight to Save the Steel Mills." *New York Review of Books* 26 (April 19, 1979): 37–40.

Machlup, Fritz. *The Economics of Sellers' Competition.* Baltimore, Md.: Johns Hopkins Press, 1952.

Mandelker, Gershon. "Risk and Return: The Case of Merging Firms." *Journal of Financial Analysis* 1 (December 1974): 303–335.

Manne, Henry G. "Mergers and the Market for Corporate Control." *Journal of Political Economy* 73 (April 1965): 110–120.

Markham, Jesse W. *Conglomerate Enterprise and Public Policy.* Boston:

Harvard University, Graduate School of Business Administration, Division of Research, 1973.

Mueller, Dennis C. "The Effects of Conglomerate Mergers." *Journal of Banking and Finance* 1 (December 1977): 315–347.

Rappaport, Alfred. "Executive Incentives vs. Corporate Growth." *Harvard Business Review* 56 (July–August 1978): 81–88.

———. "Strategic Analysis for More Profitable Acquisitions." *Harvard Business Review* 57 (July–August 1979): 99–110.

Reid, Samuel Richardson. *Mergers, Managers and the Economy.* New York: McGraw-Hill, 1968.

Salter, Malcolm I., and Weinhold, Wolf A. "Diversification via Acquisition: Creating Value." *Harvard Business Review* 56 (July–August 1978): 166–176.

Scherer, F. M. *Industrial Market Structure and Economic Performance.* Chicago, Ill.: Rand McNally, 1971.

Shenefield, John H. *Report of the Attorney General Pursuant to Section 10(c) of the Small Business Act, as Amended: Conglomerate Mergers, Small Business, and the Scope of Existing Anti-Merger Statutes.* Washington, D.C.: U.S. Department of Justice, June 20, 1979.

Sheperd, William G. *The Economics of Industrial Organization.* Englewood Cliffs, N.J.: Prentice-Hall, 1979.

Sichel, Werner. "Conglomerateness: Size and Monopoly Control." *St. John's Law Review* 44 (Spring 1970, Special Edition): 356–377.

Steiner, Peter O. *Mergers: Motives, Effects, Policies.* Ann Arbor: University of Michigan Press, 1975.

Turner, Donald E. "Corporate Mergers and Section 7 of the Clayton Act." *Harvard Law Review* 78 (May 1965): 1313–1395.

U.S. Congress, Senate, Subcommittee on Antitrust and Monopoly. *Mergers and Industrial Concentration: Hearings on Acquisitions and Mergers by Conglomerates of Unrelated Businesses.* 95th Congress, 2d session, May 12, July 27, July 28, and September 21, 1978.

U.S. Congress, Senate, Subcommittee on Antitrust, Monopoly, and Business Rights. *Mergers and Economic Concentration: Hearings on S. 600.* 96th Congress, 1st session, April 26, May 4, May 17, and May 22, 1979.

Weiss, Leonard S. "An Evaluation of Mergers in Six Industries." *Review of Economics and Statistics* 47 (May 1965): 172–181.

Winslow, John F. *Conglomerates Unlimited: The Failure of Regulation.* Bloomington: Indiana University Press, 1973.